25 ESSENTIAL LANGUAGE ARTS STRATEGIES TO HELP STRIVING READERS SUCCEED

Michael F. Opitz and Roland K. Schendel

SCHOLASTIC

New York • Toronto • London • Auckland • Sydney
Mexico City • New Delhi • Hong Kong • Buenos Aires

Dedication

To Michaela, Lindrey, and Ryer—
you mean the world to me
—RKS

To my students
—MFO

Acknowledgments

Many remarkable individuals at Scholastic contributed to this creative work and we wish to acknowledge them. The keen insights of Lois Bridges and Danny Miller helped us to think about the language arts thoughtfully, thoroughly, and critically. Danny Miller's editing brought clarity and his eye for detail and creativity shows itself in the book you are holding. We thank Sarah Morrow for her beautiful interior design and Brian LaRossa for the striking cover.

Our thanks extend to Krista Fiedler, doctoral candidate at the University of Northern Colorado, for contributing several of the lesson extension ideas and for reading and commenting on drafts of the manuscript.

We would also like to thank our families for giving us the never-ending support we needed to complete this project in a timely manner.

To all, our heartfelt thanks.

Cover Designer: Brian LaRossa
Acquiring Editor: Lois Bridges
Copy/Production Editor: Danny Miller
Interior Designer: Sarah Morrow

Copyright © 2011 by Michael F. Opitz and Roland K. Schendel
All rights reserved. Published by Scholastic Inc.
Printed in the U.S.A.
ISBN: 978-0-545-08747-6

Table of Contents

Introduction

Frustrated with the new computer and unable to comprehend the manual, I (Michael) decided to seek assistance by calling the computer company's help center. After I had resolved the problem with the help of the patient and supportive technician, I returned to my work on this book. And that's when I realized that my experience was a perfect example of what we advocate here—using all of the language processes (i.e., language arts) to facilitate our comprehension. Here's what I mean. When I was unable to decipher the printed text (*reading*) of the computer guide, I sought the help of a more knowledgeable other. Once on the phone, the computer tech asked me several questions and, as the result of *listening* to my *spoken* responses, he was able to tell me (*speaking*) what commands I needed to write. Wanting to solve my problem, I *listened* to his instructions, all the while *viewing* my computer screen to make sure that what I did worked. My ability to apply what I knew about all language processes—listening, speaking, reading, viewing, and writing—enabled me to use all of the language arts to solve my comprehension problem.

Competent language users recognize that the language arts work together. But we are concerned that children are often led to believe otherwise, that the language arts are anything but integrated. We are also concerned that children are frequently left on their own to somehow acquire the language arts that are taken for granted. For instance, children group for reading or a "literacy block" in which they are explicitly taught reading—and sometimes writing. Listening is assumed rather than taught, as are speaking and viewing.

The truth is that readers are more likely to be successful when they are shown and encouraged to use all language arts to support their comprehension efforts. That is the purpose of this book. Our goal is to help you better integrate the language arts to nurture your students' reading growth, to create *proficient, critical readers* who choose to read for a variety of purposes. As literacy demands in the new millennium continue to escalate, children need to be afforded as many opportunities as possible to critically read many different types of texts (e.g., books, wikis, blogs, and magazines) so that they can meet these demands head on, thereby functioning in the world as they know it. (Coiro, 2003; McKenna, Labbo, & Reinking, 2003; Darling-Hammond, 2010).

To accomplish our aim, we have created practical lessons, supportive text options, and lesson extensions. Make no mistake—although we have written each chapter to showcase a specific language art, every lesson shows how the remaining language arts support the one being showcased. For example, Going Graphic is a lesson that appears in Chapter 6 and focuses on viewing and understanding visual representations. A close examination of this lesson shows that students also need to use reading, writing, listening, and speaking to *go graphic*. In other words, much like a quartet in which one singer takes the spotlight and the others remain in the background to provide necessary support and harmony, the same is true with Going Graphic and the other essential strategies outlined in this book. One aspect of language arts takes center stage while the other language arts provide the support.

Just what are the language arts and how do they work together to scaffold students' learning? How can we use the language arts to meet the needs of striving readers? Chapter 1 addresses these important questions and establishes a framework for understanding each of the remaining chapters.

Chapters 2 through 6 each focus on a different language art as a vehicle for supporting striving readers. Each chapter follows a similar format. We begin by showcasing a specific language art. We provide a succinct explanation of its role in language development and offer five sound reasons for teaching it. We then provide five integrated language arts teaching strategies. Each strategy includes a description, teaching suggestions, a classroom scenario to show the activity in action, text suggestions, and lesson extensions. Chapters 2 through 6 are written as stand-alone chapters and the ideas within them can be used in a variety of ways. On the one hand, you can select any given teaching strategy to address the needs of your specific students. On the other hand, you can use the strategies across all content areas to facilitate student reading. For example, while Author's Chair is typically used to support writers, it can also be employed as a meaningful way to use listening, speaking, and writing to support readers when they engage with texts in such content areas as social studies, science, and fitness.

We are confident that this text will help you see the boundless benefits of integrating the language arts to enhance the successes of your striving readers. You will learn how to capitalize on your students' language strengths to support their reading successes! And students will learn the importance of using all language arts as they seek out and read the vast array of texts available to them.

Working With Striving Readers

Stuart's pride swells as he scoops up all of the oak building blocks from the rug around him. Hearing a "Humph," the toddler turns around. Willy stands like a statue with folded arms and a furrowed brow.

Viewing his friend's anger, Stuart says, "It is okay, Willy, we can build it todetter."

Willy's arms drop and his face relaxes a bit. "Okay, Stuart! But what does 'todetter' mean?"

"We can both do it," clarifies Stuart, and Willie beams in delight.

As this conversation shows, communication is the foundation for human behavior and interaction. Through communication, human beings share their meaning of the world around them. This exchange occurs as language abilities unfold. Understanding the components of language allows teachers to nurture the development of children as they strive to become successful language users and make sense of their world.

WHAT ARE THE LANGUAGE ARTS?

There is common agreement among literacy scholars that the language arts encompass listening, speaking, reading, writing, and visually viewing and representing (NCTE/IRA, 1996). What varies when different scholars write about the language arts is their explanation of how to best teach them. As we show in Figure 1.1, our belief is that each of the language arts can and should be used to support striving readers.

Figure 1.1. Using all of the language arts to support striving readers.

While we believe that the language arts are integrated language processes, we, like the professional literacy organizations (NCTE/IRA), also believe that each one also needs its own focus. Pulling them apart and zooming in on each of the language arts brings greater understanding and helps to clarify what it is we are trying to integrate.

Listening is the first stage of language development and continues throughout the development of all other language stages. In fact, discriminative listening begins as early as the third trimester of prenatal development (Eliot, 1999). The brain converts sounds heard in the environment into meaningful information. As development continues, children begin to discriminate the basic speech sounds that will allow them to imitate speech. Eventually, listening facilitates language play and nurtures phonological awareness. This awareness of words, syllables, and phonemes enhances speaking development as well as emergent reading skills.

But that's only the beginning! Learners continue to use listening for a variety of purposes throughout their lives, perhaps now more than ever given newer technology, which capitalizes on students' ability to critically listen. Most recently, the authors of the Common Core Standards (2010) have turned up the volume on listening by giving it equal attention to the other language arts; its importance is no longer neglected.

Speaking, the ability to orally communicate thoughts with others, requires practice, facilitation, and instruction. Children need plenty of opportunities to view how effective speakers use speaking in authentic contexts (Yellin, Blake, & DeVries, 2004). Speaking, when nurtured, helps children develop the language cuing systems (e.g., semantics, syntax, graphophonic, and pragmatics) that are important for learning to read.

As with listening, speaking is taking its rightful place in educational and political arenas alike. While many teachers have long known the importance that speaking plays in learning, it is now seen as one of several necessary communication skills in the 21st century according to educators such as Trillin & Fadel (2009) and the governing board that assembled the current Common Core Standards (2010). These educators speak to what the authors of the NCTE/IRA standards noted more than ten years ago when they wrote "much of our knowledge of language and our acquisition of literacy depends on spoken language. Any definition of language arts must therefore include helping students learn how to accomplish successfully the many functions of spoken language, such as discussing texts, making presentations, assisting visitors, or telling stories to family and friends (1996, p. 5)."

Reading emerges as children make connections between the sounds of speech and the symbols that represent those sounds and learn to decipher the code inherent to print to make meaning (Goodman, 1979). Children begin to approximate reading behaviors (e.g., pretending to read, memorizing) when reading familiar texts. They acquire print concepts such as appropriately holding a text and left-to-right progression through repeated exposure and manipulation of texts (Clay, 1979). Readers see that reading is an active, meaning-making process. To be sure, reading is a complex behavior. Few would disagree that reading begets reading and that high exposure to reading makes children's academic success possible.

Writing is also a complex mental process. The ability to write develops as the other language arts continue to develop. Nearly 50 years ago, Vygotsky (1962) argued that mental processes are augmented through using spoken *and* written language. Many children come to reading through writing, which Jane Hansen made clear in her seminal work, *When Writers Read* as did Marie Clay in her classic text, *What Did I Write?*

And let's remember that writing is a skill that is only growing in complexity in our increasingly sophisticated society, which calls on students to use writing to communicate via new technologies (e.g., texting, e-mailing, blogs, and online coursework).

Viewing involves attention to communication that is visually represented. Students view existing images (e.g., drawings, charts, graphs, photography, physical performance, computer images, television, and movies) and interpret their meaning (*visually viewing*). At other times, students show their understanding by creating an image (*visually representing*). Like Farris (2011), we recognize that visual representations are powerful influences on the daily lives of children and how they perceive the world. Therefore, understanding how to read and *interpret* what they see puts children in a better position to *evaluate* what they see. They become more sophisticated, critical, and savvy readers. Along with speaking, listening, reading, and writing, developing viewing and visually representing skills enhance language abilities and enable successful participation in society (NCTE/IRA, 1996). In fact, we see today's learners as members of the "eye" generation.

WHO ARE STRIVING READERS?

Striving readers are those resilient students who continue to work toward reading acquisition regardless of experiencing failures or hindrances (Schendel, 2010). While *struggling reader* is the term most often used in the research literature to discuss and define children who find reading difficult, we deliberately choose to use the term *striving* to stress the potential of *all* readers. We see this term as a way to view all readers with a positive and optimistic mind-set, one that sees children as showing us what they know and need to know. But perhaps children such as Lizzie, a fourth grader, say it best. In response to reading what we had written about her as a part of a larger research project, she wrote, "I would like you to change *struggling* to *striving*. It really caught my attention because it hurt my feelings."

In a sense, we are all striving readers as we continue to acquire and learn new literacies necessary for navigating our modern world. Take, for example, a recent experience I (Roland) had when ordering books for my students from a popular website. As I entered the website I paused in dismay. The titles of the icons for the online ordering had changed. Aware of the fact that I had only 20 minutes before teaching my undergraduate literacy class, I grew frustrated. I regained composure by reminding myself that I had gone through this process multiple times: "Where is the link to *Book Club Orders*? It is normally up here, on this toolbar. Is this it? *Book Clubs*?" A click of the mouse gave me my answer, "No, that's not it!" I returned to the last screen, clicked on *Orders*, and saw the familiar process for placing an order.

As this example shows, I was a striving reader because I continued to work toward understanding despite the hindrances that had unknowingly been put before me. Fortunately, I knew how to use the other language arts to assist me. And so it is with all of us. Many times, we experience setbacks in our efforts to understand our world, yet we forge ahead knowing that if we keep striving, we will eventually succeed.

WHAT ARE THE GUIDING PRINCIPLES TO SUPPORT STRIVING READERS?

Our search for essential language arts practices that teachers can use to meet the needs of striving readers led us to seven guiding principles. We drew on writings of past and current authors, models of best teaching practices, our dialogues about the essence of instruction, and our own past and current writing and teaching experiences to ground these principles. These seven guiding principles permeate the activities we describe in this book and are as follows.

1. **Use the language arts to foster critical literacy.** Critical reading is "reading in which a questioning attitude, logical analysis, and inference are used to judge the worth of text according to an established standard" (Harris & Hodges, 1995, p. 47). As the definition suggests, judgment is anything but a mere opinion. Instead, readers have some external or internal standards that help them to form their judgments. For instance, they might have additional information about the given topic, which they use to compare the current text. Critical reading calls on readers to suspend their judgments while they consider several viewpoints. It calls on readers to go beyond any one text to form their own opinions about what they have read.

    As good as critical reading is to help children acquire necessary 21st-century skills, it isn't enough; they need to develop more encompassing *critical literacy* skills as well. According to Jones (2006, p. 65), critical literacy is "an understanding that language practices and texts are always informed by ideological beliefs and perspectives whether conscious or otherwise." When teaching critical literacy, then, children are taught how to "read across the grain" (McLaughlin & DeVoogd, 2004, p. 4). They are taught to think about *why* authors write texts in a given manner. They are taught to recognize who is included as well as excluded and discuss the reasoning behind such actions.

2. **Help students understand how the language arts facilitate greater learning and reading.** Language is not a subject. It is a foundation for all learning (NCTE/IRA, 1996). All content areas rely on each of the language arts for basic and conceptual understanding. Embracing the language arts skills as the necessary tools for understanding particular areas of study nurtures student learning. As teachers focus on the teaching of the language arts as learning tools and explicitly share with students *how* they are using the different forms of language to garner understanding, learning in the content areas is more likely. Learning occurs

through the language arts (see the Common Core Standards for specific examples of how the language arts are used as tools across all content areas).

3. **Attend to the individual strengths and needs of each striving reader.** Through authentic and formative assessments, teachers can identify the strengths and needs of their striving readers. They can then use what they discover to design and teach purposeful lessons; they can create authentic and meaningful language arts activities to support continued reading growth. Without question, assessment guides instruction.

4. **Nurture/motivate student anticipation and participation.** Attending to students' interests optimizes student success. Thames, Reeves, Kazelskis, York, Boling, Newell, & Wang (2008) found that striving readers improved their reading comprehension as a result of experiencing individualized language arts instruction. Making activities relevant to the lives of the students ensures their personal connection to the learning opportunities. Furthermore, using student input promotes anticipation, participation, relevance, and opportunity for engaging reading.

5. **Employ a variety of texts.** Using a variety of texts motivates all children to become better readers (Baker & Wigfield, 1999; Edmunds & Bauserman, 2006). Using engaging and authentic texts enhances student reading comprehension through critical thinking, reading, writing, discussing, and visually representing the ideas found in a variety of texts. Going beyond books by making a variety of texts accessible and acceptable (e.g., magazines, cyber text, newspapers, video game manuals) is a sure way to honor individual student interests, strengths, and needs and to promote authenticity and students' success (Opitz & Ford, 2006).

6. **Exercise fluid and flexible grouping techniques.** Attending to students' individual strengths and needs requires fluid grouping (Opitz & Ford, 2009; Caldwell & Ford, 2002). Students can and should be taught individually through conferencing or grouped in pairs, small groups, or, at times, as a whole class depending on the purpose of each lesson and the awareness of student needs (Opitz & Ford, 2001; 2008).

7. **Plan instruction.** Any effective teaching requires thoughtful, planned instruction. Recording and stating the purpose to students guides instruction and allows them to understand the importance of the lesson. Thinking through what needs to transpire during the lesson also helps teachers to determine which specific language arts they are trying to incorporate. This deliberate integration of the language arts provides the scaffolding necessary for reading

development. Most often, teachers are expected to use their state or local school district standards, spin-offs of the NCTE/IRA Standards first published in 1996. Others are now adopting the Common Core Standards (2010). Regardless, using the Integrated Language Arts Lesson Plan Form found on page 128 reminds teachers of these seven principles.

HOW CAN TEACHERS USE THE LANGUAGE ARTS TO MEET THE NEEDS OF STRIVING READERS?

Our goal in writing this text is to encourage teachers to use essential language arts teaching strategies that incorporate all the language arts—listening, speaking, reading, writing, and viewing (visually viewing and visually representing) to further enhance their students' reading growth. The 25 essential language arts teaching strategies that make up this book (shown in Figure 1.2) do just that. They also help teachers . . .

- Nurture students' conceptual understanding through authentic learning experiences.
- Offer the insight necessary for students to understand the practical importance of language arts skills and how to apply them.
- Develop students' thinking skills and encourage use of those skills.
- Enhance students' abilities to function as literate individuals of the 21st century.

Figure 1.2 provides an overview of the language arts teaching strategies that can be used to teach striving readers. Starting with Chapter 2, each chapter showcases a different language art and offers explanations of the various activities used to teach striving readers. Remember that although a specific language art is the focus of any one chapter, the teaching strategies within that chapter incorporate the other language arts as well; they are integrated language arts lessons.

Figure 1.2. Language arts teaching strategies and the reading skills they nurture

sequence of events	academic vocabulary	social vocabulary	gathering facts	listening comprehension	determining importance	monitoring comprehension	visualizing	inferring	synthesizing	questioning	connecting	summarizing	predicting	fluency	seeing text as accessible	reading interest	Teaching Strategies	Reading Skills
•	•		•	•		•			•			•			•	•	Read-Aloud Role Play	Listening
•	•	•	•	•	•	•	•	•				•	•		•	•	Follow Along!	Listening
•			•	•		•	•	•				•	•		•	•	Directed Listening-Thinking	Listening
•		•	•		•			•		•	•	•			•	•	What's Your Perspective?	Listening
•			•		•									•	•	•	Author's Chair	Listening
•	•		•	•	•	•	•	•	•	•	•	•	•		•	•	What's on Your Mind?	Speaking
•	•		•	•	•	•	•	•	•	•		•			•	•	Pass It On!	Speaking
•			•									•		•	•	•	Scene-sational	Speaking
•	•		•	•	•	•	•	•	•	•		•	•	•	•	•	You Are the Text	Speaking
•	•		•	•	•	•	•	•	•	•	•	•			•	•	ReStory Teller	Speaking
				•										•	•	•	Paired Reading	Reading
	•		•		•						•			•	•	•	Buddy Reading	Reading
•	•		•	•	•	•	•	•	•	•	•	•	•	•	•	•	Focused Readers' Workshop	Reading
•				•		•					•			•	•	•	Cut Apart	Reading
				•		•								•	•	•	Text Slam	Reading
•	•				•		•			•	•					•	Focused Writers' Workshop	Writing
•			•	•	•	•	•	•	•	•		•		•	•	•	Read-Aloud Free Response	Writing
•	•		•		•			•		•	•	•			•	•	Two-Column Notes	Writing
•			•		•			•		•	•		•	•	•	•	Language Experience Approach	Writing
•					•		•	•		•	•				•	•	Directed Writing-Thinking (DW-TA)	Writing
•	•		•		•		•	•	•	•		•			•	•	Story Mapper	Visually Viewing and Representing
•	•		•		•		•	•	•			•			•	•	Cereal Book	Visually Viewing and Representing
	•	•	•		•		•	•	•	•		•	•		•	•	Caption Writer	Visually Viewing and Representing
•	•	•	•			•		•	•			•		•	•	•	Going Graphic	Visually Viewing and Representing
	•	•	•		•		•	•		•	•	•			•	•	Visual Scavenger Hunt	Visually Viewing and Representing

Listening Strategies

Listening is at the heart of language development. At the moment of birth, babies have approximately 12 full weeks of listening experience (Eliot, 1999). As children develop, so do their listening skills. As they interpret environmental sounds, listening becomes a vehicle for comprehension development. Due to its importance, we highlight the following five reasons for explicitly teaching listening to help striving readers reach their full reading potential.

★ *Learners develop an ability to discriminate sounds.* Listening involves the identification of the differences among sounds. This identification and discrimination leads children to the understanding that sounds are grouped together to form words.

★ *Children realize the value of listening.* Listening makes up a great percentage of a child's day, both in and out of school (Wolvin & Coakley, 1996). Expanding children's views of listening and the benefits of using good listening skills can impact *how* they use listening. For instance, listening precisely to verbal instructions has a direct impact on children's success in the classroom. They know exactly what they are to do as a result of being able to perform this type of listening.

★ *Students listen for a variety of purposes.* Listening serves many purposes.

Reading Skills	Read-Aloud Role Play	Follow Along	Directed Listening-Thinking Activity	What's Your Perspective	Author's Chair
reading interest	•	•	•	•	•
seeing text as accessible	•	•	•	•	•
fluency	•				•
predicting		•	•		
summarizing	•		•	•	
connecting	•	•	•	•	•
questioning	•	•	•	•	•
synthesizing	•	•	•	•	
inferring	•	•	•	•	
visualizing	•	•			•
monitoring comprehension	•	•	•	•	•
determining importance	•	•	•	•	
listening comprehension	•	•	•	•	
gathering facts	•	•		•	•
social vocabulary				•	•
academic vocabulary	•	•	•	•	•
sequence of events	•	•	•	•	•

Figure 2.1. Listening teaching strategies and the reading skills they nurture

Teachers can teach students to use listening to enhance their understanding of the environment, conversations, music, and stories read aloud.

★ *Listening enhances children's ability to use the other language arts.* Teaching listening allows students to follow directions, understand expectations, and make sense of verbal classroom communication. As children improve as listeners, they learn to use the same strategies to improve their command of the other language arts.

★ *Students understand the relationship between listening and reading.* Listening, like reading, is an active process. Listening and reading require the use of similar thought processes such as predicting and self-monitoring to attend to the conveyed message for the construction of meaning (Opitz, Rubin, & Erekson, 2010).

Think about how understanding the many different purposes for listening allows a striving reader to make practical connections to the many purposes for reading. When listening and reading are taught in tandem, striving readers see firsthand how their improvement as listeners supports their development as readers. They see, for example, that attending to story events when listening is similar to detecting story events when reading.

With these reasons and the connection between listening and reading comprehension in mind, we showcase five activities that use listening to enhance the reading ability of striving readers. Figure 2.1 shows these teaching strategies and the skills they elicit.

READ-ALOUD ROLE PLAY

Description: Read-Aloud Role Play provides an opportunity for striving readers to practice identifying nonverbal behaviors and to make their oral reading sound like a given character. By using the pictures and context of a specific book, readers determine the mood or behavior of a character as they develop an oral interpretation for a read-aloud. Once the personality of the character has been determined and the read-aloud has been practiced, the individual student then presents it to the class. This activity is similar to Readers Theater except here a single reader completes the entire text; it is more like a one-person show. It calls on the audience to use discriminative listening.

Discriminative Listening

Discriminative listening is the ability to know which sounds to attend to and which to ignore. It includes distinguishing among sounds, listening for specific details and ideas, and attending to nonverbal cues.

Teaching Suggestions

1. Share the purpose of the activity. Creating and performing a Read-Aloud Role Play will enhance the performers' understanding of the text and allow an audience of peers to listen discriminatively and identify different characters and their traits, which will enhance their understanding of a story.

2. Using the Read-Aloud Role Play Guide shown below, model a read-aloud to allow students to listen to what they can do to create their own and how to follow along using discriminative listening.

3. Invite students to choose a text that includes plenty of dialogue. You may want to assemble an appropriate collection in advance, such as books by Dr. Seuss, which include multiple characters.

4. Inform students that they will be reading a passage from their text to the whole class or a small group.

5. Instruct students to choose a portion of the text that will allow them to become the character(s) during their read-aloud. They will read the text in the same manner that they believe each character would actually speak the part. Accentuating character voices during their read-aloud allows the student audience to discriminate among characters and understand what is occurring in the scene performed. Post the Read-Aloud Role Play Guide for all to see. Instruct students to use it as they prepare.

Read-Aloud Role Play Guide

1. Identify and choose a text with an abundance of dialogue and multiple characters.

2. Identify and interpret the nonverbal behaviors of each character.

3. Determine the appropriate oral interpretations as you create each character voice.

4. Rehearse character voices aloud in preparation for your performance.

5. Become each character as you read aloud to your audience. Make sure to adhere to the personality traits, mannerisms, and demeanor of each character as depicted by the context of the scene and pictures.

Provide plenty of time for students to practice reading the text aloud and to create unique voices for the different characters. Circulate around the room to

★ *25 Essential Language Arts Strategies to Help Striving Readers Succeed*

monitor individual striving readers' understanding of their texts and to provide support as needed.

Invite students to perform their Read-Aloud Role Plays in small groups or sign up to perform for the whole class.

Peering into the Classroom

Roland understands that listening is one way to enhance his third graders' understanding of narrative texts and the roles that characters play. Gathering students for reading workshop, he says, "Today you will be using Read-Aloud Role Play to understand the characters and their traits in a book that you find interesting. You will use your understanding of the character voices and personalities to prepare and perform a read-aloud for your peers. Your audience will listen discriminatively to differentiate between the characters and follow along with the scene that you have chosen to read aloud. In fact, this will be a lot like what we did when we used Readers Theater."

"I will show you what to do by modeling a Read-Aloud Role Play. I want you to listen for each character as I read a scene from *Charlie Hits It Big* by Deborah Blumenthal," Roland says, pulling the book from a shelf behind him. He reads aloud a previously chosen scene from the book. With a thick French accent, he performs the part of the director who is casting Charlie for a part in a movie. Then Roland reads the movie scene as performed by Charlie in a deep voice using facial expressions and body movements to accentuate his acting.

> ### Oral Interpretation
>
> *This activity will allow students to practice self-questioning, oral interpretation, and discriminative listening. Oral interpretation involves the way that a student decides to represent characters (e.g., deep voice, British accent, etc.) and reveals student understanding of the text, characters, and character traits.*

"Could you tell the difference between the characters and follow along with the scene?" Roland asks students.

"Yes!" students respond in unison.

"I could see the French movie director and could picture Charlie acting out his part," says Arianna.

"Great!" Roland states. "I want you to do the same for your audience."

"Can we choose any story we want?" Kevin asks.

"Yes, but the text you choose should have a lot of dialogue between at least two characters." Roland answers. "You can use the Read-Aloud Role Play Guide to help you prepare," Roland says, pointing to the guide displayed on chart paper large enough for all to see.

Roland circulates around the room as students identify and choose texts to use for their read-alouds. He checks in with various striving readers to monitor their understanding of the activity. He offers support as necessary by drawing attention to the guide on display. He stops by Baseley, a striving reader, who is studying the picture book *Fancy Nancy: Bonjour Butterfly* by Jane O'Connor. The colorful text and captivating illustrations by Robin Preiss Glasser make the text a wonderful choice for this activity.

"You have chosen an incredible book for this activity, Baseley," Roland comments.

"Absolutely! I am *thrilled* to share my *extraordinary* read-aloud," states Baseley, using language taken directly from her text. She speaks in a high-pitched British accent, left toe pointed outward, left hand on hip, and chin pointed to the sky.

Picking up on Baseley's language, Roland responds, "You *are* going to captivate your audience."

After approximately 20 minutes, Roland invites students to perform their Read-Aloud Role Plays in student-chosen groups of four.

Once students are in their groups, Roland reminds them, "When you are a member of the audience, listen discriminatively to identify the characters, their traits, and to make sense of the scene performed." He moves around the room to listen in on read-aloud performances.

At the end of the read-aloud performances, Roland says, "Remember, attending to the voice and personalities of each character allows you to understand character traits. Not only that, listening discriminatively to a read-aloud performance allows you to identify different characters, understand each character's role in a story, and understand what is going on in the story. Both reading aloud and listening discriminatively will help you become better readers by developing your reading comprehension *and* listening comprehension."

Text Suggestions

- *Charlie Hits It Big* by Deborah Blumenthal
- *Fancy Nancy: Bonjour, Butterfly* by Jane O'Connor
- *I'm Not Invited?* by Diana Cain Bluthenthal
- *Lilly's Purple Plastic Purse* by Kevin Henkes

- *Purplicious* by Victoria Kann and Elizabeth Kann
- *Sipping Spiders Through a Straw* by Kelly DiPucchio
- *This Little Piggy's Book of Manners* by Kathryn Madeline Allen

Extension Ideas

★ Many students enjoy speaking in strange or funny voices. Give them the opportunity to manipulate their voices and match them with specific characters. Using a list of characters written on the board, students first share voice options for each character by reading practiced sections of text aloud to the class. The class decides which voice matches each character best. Second, having honed in on the voice for each character, students have an opportunity to try out for the part after having practiced a character of interest.

★ Another way to develop students' discriminative listening is to provide them with practice listening for specific details in a text. A fun way to do so is to use the book *Sipping Spiders Through a Straw,* which features creepy monster songs set to familiar tunes. Before the activity, choose about five different pictures from the book that include details in the song and make a copy of each for students to view. Sing the songs from the book and have them match their pictures to the songs by listening discriminatively for the details.

FOLLOW ALONG!

Description: In Follow Along!, students listen for details in a read-aloud to see how a story unfolds and to identify each event in sequence. They determine the place, object, person, or animal that a poem depicts. With poetry, students may be asked to think about and sketch or write the details that help them identify what the poem describes. With practice, students learn to use *precise listening* to understand poems about people, places, or things that they are familiar with and then graduate to understanding more complex poems depicting ideas or concepts.

The ability to use precise listening to understand poetry read aloud is then used to scaffold a striving reader's ability to comprehend poems read independently.

Precise Listening

Precise listening is the ability to pay attention to what is being shared and to ascertain details. It includes skills such as associating words with meaning, deducing meaning of words from context, recalling details, following directions, and recognizing multiple characters.

Teaching Suggestions

1. Select a poetry text that contains several poems that do not explicitly state the object or subject of each poem. It may be necessary to omit the title of the poem or leave out a line or word to force students to listen to the details of the poem and identify what is being described.

2. Practice reading the selected poems before reading them to students.

3. Share the purpose of the activity with students—to use precise listening skills to identify and understand the details of a poem to identify what the poem is describing. Explain that the ability to use precise listening to understand a poem during a read-aloud can then be used to understand poetry that is read independently.

4. Model the process for students. Read a selected poem aloud and share your thoughts about what the poem is about. Read the poem a second time and model note taking and the identification of important details.

5. Read a new poem aloud to the students. Instruct them to listen to the first reading and pay attention to the details presented in the poem to identify what the poem is about.

6. Read the text aloud a second time. Invite students to consider and sketch or write important details that help them to identify what the poem describes.

7. Invite students to reveal what the poem is about through writing, turn-talk-and-listen, or during a whole-class share.

Peering into the Classroom

Marina understands the value of using poetry to enhance her second graders' reading comprehension. In fact, she reads poetry aloud to students daily. Now she intends to use poetry to teach students how to use precise listening and how they can use the same skills to understand poetry that they read themselves. Marina decides to use Follow Along! to accomplish this goal. She selects and practices reading aloud several poems about familiar animals.

Pointing to the purpose she has written on the board for all to see, Marina begins the lesson saying, "This morning I am going to show you how to listen precisely to identify the important details in a text that is read aloud. Identifying important details in a poem will allow you to understand what the poem describes. Understanding how to identify important details when listening will help you understand how to do the same when you are reading on your own."

Marina shows students the cover of the poetry book she has prepared for this lesson and reads the title aloud. She shares, "This is *In the Swim* by Douglas Florian. It is a collection of poems about real underwater creatures. I will show you what you will be doing by reading a poem aloud two times. After I read the poem the first time, I will pause to think about the details I hear. The second time I read the poem, I will draw or write details that I think might be important."

Marina reads a poem about jellyfish. She omits the title since it is the only portion of the text that explicitly reveals what the poem is describing. She pauses after the first reading and thinks aloud by saying, "I heard the details *umbrella* and *peanut butter*, which I think will help me figure out what the poem is about. Let me see if I can figure this out with the second read-aloud."

Marina reads the poem aloud a second time. She stops halfway through and, while writing a few words, thinks aloud by saying, "Oh, *tentacles* that *paralyze*—I am pretty sure that I know what it is now. I just need to finish the second reading to make sense of the part about peanut butter." Marina completes the read-aloud and nods, exclaiming, "Yes! The poem is about a jellyfish because it is *umbrella-shaped*, has tentacles, and its name goes with peanut butter." She shows the title of the poem to students to verify her conclusions.

"Now it is your turn," says Marina. "I will read another poem and you will use precise listening to identify the important details that will help you figure out what the words in the poem describe. I will read the poem aloud two times and you will do just as I did. The first time through, just listen precisely. During the second reading, you can think and draw or write the details that you hear. We'll then check with the book to see if your conclusions match those of the author."

Marina reads a new poem about a starfish and omits only the title, which names the creature. She decides to include the word *star* that is found in the text to serve as a scaffold for helping students to identify the subject of the poem. She reminds students to just listen to the first reading. Before reading the poem aloud the second time, she encourages students to record the details that they hear while listening. She pauses for a minute after the second reading to allow students to ponder what the poem might be about. She then asks, "So what do you think? What's the poem describing?"

"A starfish!" students holler in unison.

Background Knowledge

Using texts about topics that are familiar to students allows teachers to scaffold student understanding by adding new knowledge to an existing knowledge base.

Sharing the Purpose

Stating the purpose and displaying it on the board for repeated reference is one way to keep many students focused on the lesson.

"You are very precise listeners!" Marina exclaims. Marina closes the lesson by saying, "Remember, in much the same way that you use precise listening to identify important details, you can also use precise reading to make sense of a written text when you read. Try it today when you are reading your self-selected books during independent reading time."

Text Suggestions

- *Animal Poems* by Valerie Worth
- *Feeding the Sheep* by Leda Schubert
- *Hippopotamus Stew and Other Silly Animal Poems* by Joan Horton
- *In the Swim* by Douglas Florian
- *Like People* by Ingrid and Dieter Schubert
- *The Puzzle of the Platypus* by Jack Myers
- *Stand Tall, Abe Lincoln* by Judith St. George

Extension Ideas

★ Detailed Defense is another activity that helps students develop precise listening. In this courtroom simulation, students listen for details in the book being read aloud because they may be called to be a witness in a mock trial. One person takes on the role of lawyer after seeing the role modeled by the teacher. The "judge" (usually the teacher) uses the book to check for accuracy as the lawyer drills the witnesses on what they heard. The witnesses assume the role of bystanders and report the details as they heard them when listening to the text.

★ Say and Sketch is a group activity that focuses on following precise directions. In groups of four, pick one student to be the direction giver. Give the direction givers a simple drawing and instruct them not to show it to the other group members. Give each of the other students a blank piece of a paper and a pencil. The direction giver describes the simple drawing while the other group members draw the details on their paper. The object is for the group members to precisely listen to the verbal instructions in order to draw the design accurately.

DIRECTED LISTENING-THINKING ACTIVITY (DL-TA)

Description: The Directed Listening-Thinking Activity (DL-TA) is intended to nurture students' ability to make meaning and develop story structure as a text is read aloud by the teacher. The teacher typically reads the title of the text and asks students to predict what will happen in the story. Students also create questions that they think will be answered after hearing the story. The teacher reads the story aloud, stopping at certain points to allow students to verify predictions, answer questions, and pose new questions.

Developing an extensive listening vocabulary and helping students use predicting make DL-TA a powerful strategy for aiding students in understanding oral and written discourse. It enables a striving reader to construct meaning based on information presented by others. It is one way for striving readers to use *strategic listening* to make sense of a spoken message or a text that has been read aloud.

> ### Strategic Listening
>
> Strategic listening is the ability to use listening to gain understanding of the intended meaning of a message. It includes skills such as listening for understanding, realizing when comprehension is breaking down, identifying a speaker's intended message, and remembering a message for future use.

Teaching Suggestions

1. Determine the material to use for the activity, which may include a written text, an audio recording, an oral story, a lecture, or a DVD.
2. Prepare the reading, story, or presentation.
3. Make the activity meaningful to the striving readers by sharing the purpose of the activity—to interact with the text by thinking about what has been read and to pose questions and make predictions that may be answered later in the text.
4. Preview the text with the students.
5. Allow time for students to make predictions and pose questions.
6. Present the information to students and stop at designated points to have them confirm predictions and identify answers to their questions. Have them create new predictions and questions for the succeeding section of text either as a whole group, in pairs, or individually.
7. Read or present the information up to the next designated stopping point. Have students confirm or create predictions and answer and develop questions as done previously.

8. Share the text in this manner until a final stopping point is reached. Invite students to discuss the text, assess predictions, and seek answers to their questions.

Peering into the Classroom

Paul regularly holds individual conferences with his second graders during independent silent reading. All of this conferencing has helped him see that several students need to learn how to be more strategic readers. He decides to use the Directed Listening-Thinking Activity to scaffold their understanding of how to be strategic readers. That is, he will use listening comprehension and show them how it connects to reading comprehension.

Paul calls students together, and once they are settled, states, "Today we are going to do an activity that will help you use predicting and questioning to think about what you are reading. Let's try using listening to make predictions and ask questions."

Paul reaches into his pocket and pulls out a text about the eating habits of frogs. He reads the title aloud and shows students several of the pictures in the section he will read to them. Paul asks students to make some predictions and to pose some questions. After students suggest a few predictions and questions, Paul begins reading aloud, stopping occasionally for students to assess the accuracy of their predictions, adjust them as necessary, and to create new ones for the coming text. He also provides time to answer their questions and for them to pose new questions.

> ### Formative Assessment: Conferencing
>
> *Conferencing with students allows teachers to identify common skills that students need to learn. These can be taught using a whole-class lesson.*

After completing the read-aloud in this manner, Paul states to students, "What you just did as listeners is what you can also do as readers. As you read, you make predictions and pose questions. You then read a little and stop to check your predictions and questions to make sense of what you are reading."

Before Paul can even issue an invitation for students to give it a try, Danny declares, "I am ready to try this with my book. I have some things that I would like to find out." Paul takes his cue from Danny, stating, "And that is exactly what you get to do right now. All of you will now read your books and practice making predictions and posing questions to help you make sense of what you are reading."

Text Suggestions

- *Americans Who Tell the Truth* by Robert Shetterly
- *Bebé Goes to the Beach* by Susan Middleton Elya
- *The Best Story* by Eileen Spinelli
- *Lady Liberty* by Doreen Rappaport
- *The Rabbit and the Turtle* by Eric Carle
- *This Is Your Life Cycle* by Heather Lynn Miller
- *Well Witched* by Frances Hardinge

Extension Ideas

★ Two aspects of strategic listening are identifying the speaker's intended message and synthesizing/drawing conclusions. A good book to use while practicing both of these strategic listening skills is *The Rabbit and the Turtle.* In this book, Eric Carle retells Aesop's Fables, with the moral of the fable told in a different color at the bottom of each one-page story. Read each story to the class but omit the moral. Ask children to get into partners and write their own one-sentence moral for each fable. They can then share their morals orally with the class and explain their reasoning.

★ Another way to listen strategically to gain understanding is to practice summarizing. Doreen Rappaport's beautifully illustrated *Lady Liberty* is a book that works well for developing this skill. The book is written from the point of view of ten people instrumental in bringing the Statue of Liberty to America. Because the book is rather lengthy, it may be best to break the reading down into different sections. After listening to all the different points of view, have students secretly choose to be one of the people in the book. They can stand in front of the class and say a few sentences, pretending they are the character, giving clues from what they heard during the text reading. The rest of the class can guess who they are.

WHAT'S YOUR PERSPECTIVE?

Description: What's Your Perspective? encourages striving readers to listen for bias in a read-aloud, speech, discussion, or presentation and then do the same when they are reading on their own. Students are taught to listen critically and pay special attention to loaded words (Opitz & Zbaracki, 2004). Words may be used to exemplify or embellish the grandeur of an object or idea. For instance, a commercial might vividly describe the graphics of a new video game using powerful word choices like "life-like animation" or "instant 3-D character movements" but neglect to point out the game's limitations (e.g., single-player mode, no way to mute the sound when needed).

What's Your Perspective? can also help students identify words a speaker uses that reveal that person's point of view. For example, the speaker might use the pronouns *I* or *you* repeatedly. The use of *I* tells a listener that the story is told in first person and suggests bias toward the speaker. On the other hand, a message told using the word *you* tends to project the message onto the listener. This may be the case in advertisements where the message is intended to get the listener to buy a particular product. In either case, these tendencies reveal the speaker's point of view. *Critical listening* allows listeners to judge the value of the message and establish their own perspective.

> ### *Critical Listening*
>
> *Critical listening is the ability to analyze and evaluate a message. It includes skills such as evaluating a speaker's message, identifying the speaker's bias or perspective, understanding the speaker's implied message, understanding relevant and irrelevant information, and distinguishing fact from opinions.*

Teaching Suggestions

1. Choose a story that focuses on an interesting or perhaps controversial subject and practice reading the story aloud several times.

2. Determine what you might have students do during your oral reading to keep them engaged (e.g., two-column notes, journal reflections, free response).

3. Share the purpose of the activity: to listen critically for the author's perspective and to document the author's ideas by taking notes before, during, and after the reading.

4. Elicit students' background knowledge by asking them several open-ended questions before reading aloud a book, allowing time for students to think through their answers before asking for volunteers to share their thoughts with their neighbors. Sample questions may include:

- *What is the relationship between people and animals on this planet?*
- *What is the role of zoos?*

5. Pause to check student understanding during your read-aloud by providing plenty of time for whole-class, small-group, or paired discussions. Encourage written responses to better ensure that all students show accountability for their listening.

6. Invite students to identify the perspectives of those involved in the story (e.g., authors, characters, and audience) and whether they think any bias exists in the reading.

7. Reread the story aloud and have students identify segments of text that support their identification of bias.

8. Invite students to practice listening critically to identify differing perspectives and bias in other texts during silent reading and guided reading groups.

Peering into the Classroom

Terri wants her striving fifth-grade readers to be critical listeners. She regularly reads nonfiction texts aloud to her students to teach critical listening as a tool for students to determine authors' perspectives when reading.

> ### Nonfiction Texts
>
> *Nonfiction texts offer ample opportunities to develop critical listening skills such as identifying author's bias or perspective, and identifying relevant and irrelevant information.*

Based on her students' interests, Terri reads about particular animals or insects. She also finds that texts about controversial subjects like racism, discrimination, and environmental consciousness are wonderful topics to read aloud to develop critical listening.

Today Terri is reading *Knut: How One Little Polar Bear Captivated the World.* She chose it because of the controversial subject matter concerning global warming and natural selection. Prior to reading the story to students, Terri engages them in a discussion about these topics, which they have studied previously in class. With their background knowledge brought forward, Terri informs students that the text provides a few differing perspectives regarding the topic of natural selection. The purpose is for the class to listen critically for perspectives regarding both topics and the authors' use of loaded words.

Due to the length of the story, Terri decides to break it up into manageable chunks by requesting that students respond to the text in their free writing journals at several points throughout the read-aloud. She begins to read, stopping several times for three to four minutes to give her students time to respond in writing or drawings. When she stops for her students to reflect, she either models the reflection process herself or strolls around the room to peek at and formatively assess student responses. Following the reading, Terri says, "Turn-talk-and-listen to a neighbor about how you used critical listening." Terri adds, "Try to make specific references to the text to back up your arguments and comments." She rereads portions of the text to clarify some points made by the students and to emphasize the importance of critical listening. Terri concludes the lesson saying, "Listening critically allows you to understand messages more clearly and make informed decisions and judgments. You also do the same when reading. Just as you do when listening critically, you can read critically to understand and evaluate written texts and make decisions about whether you want to accept or reject the information."

> **Formative Assessment: Class Discussion**
>
> *Discussion allows Terri and her students to assess one another's understanding of the text and their use of critical thinking skills.*

Text Suggestions

- *Back of the Bus* by Aaron Reynolds
- *The Earth and I* by Frank Asch
- *Knut: How One Little Polar Bear Captivated the World* by Juliana, Isabella, and Craig Hatkoff, and Dr. Gerald R. Uhlich
- *Planting the Trees of Kenya* by Claire A. Nivola
- *Surprising Sharks* by Nicola Davies
- *Tin Lizzie* by Allan Drummond
- *Woolbur* by Leslie Helakoski

Extension Ideas

★ Critical listening involves evaluating the speaker's message and identifying his or her perspective. *Tin Lizzie* is a useful text to help students identify and discuss perspectives. It raises questions about our dependence on cars and their effect on the environment. After reading the book to the class, ask students to identify the message they think the author is trying to convey. Reread different parts from the book and ask students to discuss whether they agree or disagree with the message and to explain their reasoning.

★ Critical listening includes identifying relevant and irrelevant information. Before you read a book such as *Planting the Trees of Kenya*, write ten details on the board. Include essential and non-essential details drawn from the text. Ask students to read the details before they listen to you read it aloud. Read the book aloud, stressing the details on the board when you come to them in the book. Ask students to write the details from the list that they feel are the most relevant. Have them compare the details they chose with their partners. Ask a few partner groups to share out with the class, and hold a discussion on what makes a detail relevant or irrelevant.

AUTHOR'S CHAIR

Description: Author's Chair, a term coined by Donald Graves and Jane Hansen in 1983, allows young writers to share ideas and to build their writing efficacy. More than that, it allows young writers to gather feedback from peers as they navigate the writing process.

Author's Chair also provides an opportunity to model appropriate listening behaviors and to explicitly teach listening strategies. Finally, it provides an excellent vehicle for students to use *appreciative listening* to identify powerful uses of classmates' writing (e.g., cadence and rhythm, word choice, sentence beginnings). Learning to listen appreciatively helps students when reading their own and others' texts.

> ### Appreciative Listening
>
> *Appreciative listening is the ability to use listening to appreciate oral style. It includes skills such as recognizing the power of language, appreciating oral interpretations, and understanding the power of imagination.*

Teaching Suggestions

1. Explain to students the purpose for appreciative listening—to recognize the power of language and understand the power of imagination. Appreciate listening helps to make reading more enjoyable and memorable.

2. After providing time for students to write during writers' workshop, invite volunteers to share their work by reading it aloud.

3. Ask the audience members to explain the appropriate listening behaviors they will exhibit.

4. Encourage the reader to state his or her expectations for the listening audience. Invite the reader to give the audience a clear purpose for listening to the reading. For example, a student might say, "I would like you to listen for how I use sentence beginnings. Do I begin every sentence in a different way to keep you interested?"

5. Be prepared to offer a model response after the reading such as, "The unique use of sentence beginnings helped your writing to flow. You used transition words such as *first*, *then*, and *finally*." Allow plenty of time for students to comment.

6. Inform students that listening appreciatively during Author's Chair will help them use language in their writing that others may appreciate when listening to *them* read their compositions aloud during Author's Chair.

Peering into the Classroom

Phil believes that his fourth graders can learn to use appreciative listening to become better readers. Therefore, he decides to teach them *how* to listen appreciatively as peers share their written work in Author's Chair.

At the start of writers' workshop, he comments, "Today, as you volunteer to share your writing, we are going to focus on how to appreciate what you hear and to explain what you appreciate. Being aware of what you appreciate when listening can help you to do the same when you are reading and writing. For example, you might really like the way someone uses sentence openers to draw you in as a listener. You can then purposefully use the same technique in your writing and be on the lookout for it when reading other texts, which will make your reading more enjoyable and memorable."

The workshop progresses in typical fashion, with students writing and conferring with Phil. At their designated sharing portion of the writers' workshop, Phil asks students to prepare themselves for sharing and listening appreciatively by turning their seats toward the author's chair. He asks, "What will your listening behaviors look like while the author reads?"

James begins, "It is a good idea to look at the author."

"Yes, unless we are visualizing and listening with our eyes closed," adds Veronica.

"When I read, I love it when the audience is very still and silent. It makes me think that they are listening to my every word," offers Sarah. Many students nod in agreement.

"Beautiful, sounds like you are ready for sharing. Do I have a volunteer?" Allie stands and walks to the throne-like chair that serves as "Author's Chair."

"I want you to listen to my writing for how I used words at the beginnings of sentences. Do they make you appreciate what you hear? Do you want to keep listening? Or do you hear too many sentences start the same way?" Allie says, lifting her notebook up to read aloud. After Allie reads, Phil models an appropriate response, stating, "I enjoyed listening to your writing because your sentence beginnings were different." Several students take his lead and share their appreciation for her sentence beginnings and go so far as to mention some specific words they heard. Allie beams.

Phil wraps up the workshop by explaining, "Listening appreciatively allows you to recognize the power of language and understand the power of imagination. You can do the same while reading. You can appreciate the way the author uses words to keep you interested."

Text Suggestions

- *Dirty Joe the Pirate* by Bill Harley
- *Drive* by Nathan Clement
- *Henry's Freedom Box* by Ellen Levine
- *The Jupiter Stone* by Paul Owen Lewis
- *Max's Dragon* by Kate Banks
- *Mother's Song* by Ellin Greene
- *There's a Crocodile Under My Bed!* by Ingrid and Dieter Schubert

Dialogue

Reading aloud texts that have an abundance of dialogue enables students to see how authors use dialogue and how they vary words that signal talking (e.g., said, bellowed, replied, sighed).

Extension Ideas

★ Cadence and rhythm play a large role in listening appreciatively. One book that has a natural, rolling rhythm that you can't help but tap your toe or snap your fingers to is *Possum Come a-Knockin'* by Nancy Van Laan. Rehearse reading the book aloud to learn the rhythm. Then get ready to hear students burst into clapping, tapping, and drumming as they match the beat of the words while you read. Ask students to rate it on a five-star scale, explaining their choice.

★ Recognizing the feeling or the mood that is evoked by a book is a skill that goes along with appreciative listening. *Henry's Freedom Box* by Ellen Levine is a book in which the author's words allow the reader to feel the pain that Henry feels as his early life is recounted and to rejoice with him when he escapes to freedom in an unusual way. Ask students to listen for the feeling or mood in different parts of the story. Stop periodically and allow them to turn-talk-and-listen with a partner about how the author and illustrator use words and pictures to convey feeling.

CHAPTER 3

LISTENING SPEAKING READING WRITING VIEWING

Speaking Strategies

Speech nurtures the thought process. Think about it. We often make sense of experiences, new knowledge, and concepts by *talking* them through. Seeing the value of talking makes teachers more inclined to structure time to build students' oral language skills. It is also an effective way to boost striving readers' skills. In truth, there are five good reasons for establishing a positive talk environment.

★ *Readers take ownership of ideas by putting their thoughts into spoken words.* Striving readers make concepts memorable by expressing them. Talking about abstract concepts makes them more tangible. By putting elusive ideas into their own words, children give themselves "handles to hold on to" (Cullinan, 1993, p. 2).

★ *Learners clarify thoughts as they talk about them.* Talking is one way to clarify and extend understanding of a topic. Through talk, learners organize their ideas. Having practiced sorting out their ideas through oral language, learners are more likely to do the same when reading (and listening, writing, and viewing).

★ *Confidence and command of language use increase.* The increase in confidence and the ensuing increase in speaking ability provide the language skills necessary

Reading Skills	What's on Your Mind?	Pass It On!	Scene-sational	You Are the Text	ReStory Teller
reading interest	●	●	●	●	●
seeing text as accessible	●	●	●	●	●
fluency			●	●	
predicting	●			●	
summarizing	●	●		●	●
connecting	●	●	●	●	●
questioning	●	●		●	●
synthesizing	●	●		●	●
inferring				●	●
visualizing	●	●	●	●	●
monitoring comprehension	●	●	●	●	●
determining importance	●	●	●	●	●
listening comprehension	●	●	●	●	●
gathering facts		●	●	●	●
social vocabulary	●	●		●	
academic vocabulary	●	●		●	●
sequence of events	●	●	●	●	●

Figure 3.1. Speaking teaching strategies and the reading skills they nurture

for learning to understand written language through reading. Children with good speaking skills become better readers. What Walter Loban discovered years ago (1963) still rings true in the new millennium: Learning to read is easier for children with highly developed oral language.

★ *Discussing texts facilitates understanding.* Talking after reading allows striving readers to share their ideas about the text. By sharing their own ideas and listening to the ideas of others, striving readers clarify and heighten their understanding.

★ *Talk allows for formative assessment.* Listening to striving readers talk enables teachers to hear and better understand student thinking. They can also gain insight into readers' comprehension and reading interests. Once identified, teachers can use this information to plan meaningful learning experiences and to select reading materials that will motivate readers.

With these reasons in mind, we showcase five ways to use speaking to enhance reading ability. Figure 3.1 shows these activities and the skills they elicit.

WHAT'S ON YOUR MIND?

Description: Conversational talk is significantly different from a focused discussion. In a conversation, the manner of speaking is informal and often unstructured. Talk flows from topic to topic and speakers may decide to add anything that is on their mind. Talking usually occurs among a small number of people, allowing each the freedom to express ideas and practice talking.

What's on Your Mind? is one way to enhance conversational language. Students begin the day by gathering on the floor. Once seated, they face a neighbor, legs crossed, knee to knee. One student explains something that has been on his or her mind lately (e.g., an interesting experience or a troubling encounter) while the other listens. They then reverse roles. The main point is that students get to use conversational language to share thinking with interested peers. When first providing time for conversational talk, teachers ask students to wait for their partner to finish speaking before responding. Students are then taught how to take turns in a conversation to clarify, question, and support one another's ideas, as necessary. The teacher points out that clarifying and questioning are the same strategies that proficient readers use while reading.

Teaching Suggestions

1. Make sure students have plenty of room to assemble on the floor. If space is limited, you may want to have students turn-talk-and-listen with a neighbor at their desks.

2. Tell students that this activity will happen daily or weekly as signaled on the class schedule (you can use an icon of a head with a speech bubble).

3. Explain the purpose of practicing conversational talk and how it connects to reading. The purpose is to allow students to talk freely with others so that they can practice clarifying spoken ideas and questioning what they hear, which prepares them to do the same when reading.

4. Prepare students to face their conversation partner and sit knee to knee.

5. Invite students to talk about *anything* that is on their minds. Remind them that their sharing needs to be appropriate for the classroom.

6. Tell students that while their partner is talking, they need to show active listening by looking at the speaker and offering nonverbal cues. They also need to think what is being shared and decide if they need any clarification, or want to offer a supporting comment. Express the importance for both students to have the opportunity to speak and listen.

7. Remind students that clarifying and questioning are two strategies that they will also use when reading.

Peering into the Classroom

As the students stream into the classroom, conversation erupts. This has become a common occurrence for Michaela's first graders. Understanding her students' need to share their thinking, the importance for practicing talk to nurture their listening skills, and the relationship conversational speaking has to conversations readers have with authors while reading, Michaela decides to offer more scheduled opportunities for her students to practice their conversational skills. She decides to use the What's on Your Mind? activity with her students.

Michaela plans to offer the activity at the beginning of the school day. She rearranges the desks to allow the entire class to sit in a circle on the floor. Starting the activity on the floor will allow her to model the talk behaviors, to have pairs of students model talk for the rest of the class to see and hear, and to have individual students talk with the whole group after talking with their partners.

Michaela calls the first graders to the group meeting area and has them sit on the floor. She points to the icon on the schedule that shows that it is time for What's on Your Mind? and explains, "The purpose of this activity is to allow you the opportunity to talk freely with a partner about what is on your mind. Talking provides you with valuable practice clarifying ideas and questioning what is said, which prepares you to do the same while reading what an author has written. These strategies help you to understand messages as a listener and a reader."

Michaela takes a place in the circle with her first graders. As she asks her students to swivel on their bottoms to face a neighbor, she models the action. Jeremy raises his hand and asks, "Can I talk to two neighbors?"

"If one purpose of this activity is to give you each practice talking freely, what would be an appropriate answer to Jeremy's question?"

Sarah offers a response, "Well, if we want more time to practice, then we don't want to sit there listening the whole time. We want to get more turns."

"That's a good point, Sarah," replies Michaela. "How many people should be in a group for you to get as much talk practice as possible?"

"Just two people," declares Jeremy, with a smile.

Michaela continues, "Okay, what do you think you can talk about if we call this activity What's on Your Mind? and we have been using the term *free talk*?"

"Anything we want!" many of the first graders chime in unison.

"That's correct," says Michaela. "The key is that your talk must be appropriate and respectful of your listener and our learning environment. You also need to be aware that according to our daily schedule, you may have only a few minutes to practice talking," Michaela explains while pointing to the schedule shown on the whiteboard. "Remember that you also get the opportunity to practice your listening behaviors while your partner is talking. What can you do to show that you are listening?"

"We can look at our partner," declares Claire.

"We could also give silent signals like nodding or smiling to show that we are listening," adds Trenton.

Modeling

Modeling conversational talk makes the expectations for the activity explicit. The teacher can model the expected behaviors with a student, or a pair of students can volunteer to perform a conversational volley while their classmates experience the process.

Prompting

The teacher purposefully uses talk to prompt students to consider possible answers to the questions of peers. Doing so helps students to see that they can think through the questions of others to arrive at an answer.

"Yes, you need to do both of these," Michaela says. "But you also need to think about what the speaker is saying. You will need to decide if you need clarification."

"Are there any questions before we begin?" asks Michaela. Nearly every first grader in the class shoots a hand into the air. "Yes, Keegan?"

"We get to talk about *anything*?" As Keegan asks his question, all of the other hands reveal the same inquiry by lowering. All eyes are wide.

Sensing the enthusiasm that their free talk is about to erupt, Michaela nods her head yes, and asks, "How loud should your voices be?"

"Loud enough for our neighbor to hear but not so loud that our voice disturbs other people," shares Maisy.

"Absolutely, that was a great explanation," affirms Michaela.

Without a moment's notice, the class begins speaking excitedly. Given their excitement at having the opportunity, Michaela is pleasantly surprised that the volume of the free-talk environment is close to acceptable. It may take some guidance on her part to help them adjust the noise level, but they don't need Michaela to inspire their participation.

After the groups have had time to talk, Michaela reconvenes the whole group to close the lesson. She states, "This activity will build your ability to have similar conversations with authors while you read. You will be prepared to question and make sense of the text by supporting it with ideas of your own." Michaela finishes the lesson stating, "So today when you are reading, think about the conversation you are having with the author."

> ### Grouping
>
> *Small groups allow each person in the group as much free-talk practice as possible. Pairs work particularly well for short periods of time.*

Text Suggestions

- *Almost* by Richard Torrey
- *Don't Forget Your Etiquette!* by David Greenberg
- *Food Rules!* by Bill Haduch
- *It's Disgusting and We Ate It!* by James Solheim
- *Max and the Dumb Flower Picture* by Martha Alexander
- *Once Upon a Saturday* by Leslie Lammle
- *Science Warriors* by Sneed B. Collard III

Extension Ideas

★ A positive talk environment in the classroom begins with practicing conversational language. Once students have had practice with open topic conversations, you can suggest that they have a conversation about a common text. Read *Almost* by Richard Torrey to the class. Tell students that they will be following the same structure as *What's On Your Mind?* but that the conversation will start with their thoughts on the book. State that they may talk about what the boy in the story can almost do or what things they can almost do. Another good text for this is a poem out of David Greenberg's *Don't Forget Your Etiquette!*, as the poems are funny and relatable.

★ To make the conversation with an author seem more accessible, gather several books that you know students have enjoyed. Have them pair up by book, and then create Popsicle stick puppets of themselves and the author of the book. Have them review the book and write down two comments for the author about the characters, the plot, the setting, and so on. Ask them to also write down any questions they have. Students can then take turns sharing the comments or the questions using the puppets, with one student being themselves, and the other acting as the author. The student acting as the author tries to answer the questions as they think the author might. Encourage the students to use the questions and comments as a starting point to the conversation, and stress they don't need to limit their puppet conversation to what has been written down. Switch roles so the other student has a chance to be the author. To wrap up this activity, explain that we have similar conversations with authors in our heads when we read.

PASS IT ON!

Description: What makes a text great? What compels a reader to want to share a story that they have read? The reasons are many and are particular to individual readers. Each has different interests and views of the world that are molded by past and current experiences. For one reader, a text may be seen as great because of the characters. For another, the same text may be great because of the author's word choice. Readers' unique perspectives make sharing their reading a personal endeavor.

In any case, two benefits result from speaking about texts. One is that a striving reader makes greater sense of a text by considering and highlighting the value the text might hold for others. The processes for determining what to share and how to speak about the text to others bring new understanding to self and readers. A second benefit is that speaking about texts exposes students to new texts that may be of interest.

Building Background

Striving readers' interest in certain topics is often limited by a lack of personal experiences. Purposeful talk is one way to broaden their experiences.

Pass It On! offers one way for striving readers to expand their personal understanding of what makes a text great. It helps them broaden their interests and nurtures their desire to read more. This activity follows an in-class silent reading period. Initially, the teacher entices students to read new texts by modeling a process for sharing. For instance, the teacher may talk briefly about an action-packed scene, describe personal reactions while reading, or simply pose a compelling question about a given text. After teacher modeling, students talk about their texts in a similar manner. Doing so enables a striving reader to develop a greater understanding of the text and to be seen as the reading "expert" of that text.

Teaching Suggestions

1. Show the power of text talks by posing a leading question and statement that partially reveals the story of a given book. For example, "How does a scrawny young boy become a great wizard? Emrys' life is changed by a horrific accident. The journey that follows takes him on unbelievable adventures with incredible characters. Explore how the greatest wizard of all time found out about his magic powers in *The Lost Years of Merlin*."

2. Inform the students that the purpose of the text talk is to broaden their exposure to a variety of interesting texts, and to share the texts with others through talking.

3. Tell students that one of the best times to pass the text to others is directly after silent reading.

4. Explain that each day a few volunteers will get to do Pass It On! by following the procedure displayed in Figure 3.2.

While the students share, write their text titles and where they can be found on a chart large enough for all to see. Doing so enables all interested students to access the text.

Pass It On!

1. Read silently.

2. Think about what you would like to share with others as you read.

3. Write what you will say in your reflection log during and after reading.

4. Sign up on the class schedule if you would like to share with others.

5. In turn, Pass It On!

Figure 3.2. Procedures for Pass It On! *text talks*

Peering into the Classroom

Michael works daily to nurture his striving readers' understanding of what they read. He has led many of his second graders to engaging texts by doing the Pass It On! activity throughout the first few weeks of school. After viewing book talks online at digitalbooktalk.com and nancykeane.com/booktalks/title.htm, and reading about book talks in *Books Kids Will Sit Still For* by Judy Freeman, he has decided to pose an enticing leading question followed by several statements that partially reveal the story.

Michael informs his students that there are a wide variety of texts that they might find interesting. He also tells his students, "The power of a text talk is twofold. First, when I prepare the sharing of an interesting text, I become a better reader by developing a greater understanding of the text. Second, a thoughtful text talk will inspire others to read it themselves, which will make them better readers. So today while you read, think whether there is anything in your book that you would want to share with others." Michael then invites his students to read silently.

The second graders scatter about the room for the daily silent reading time. Some lie under desks. Others nestle in squishy bean bags or sprawl with heads propped on stuffed reading animals. While most are in "the reading zone" (Atwell, 2006), a few pace before the many bookshelves, thumb through racks of magazines, or sift through newspaper displays in their search for compelling texts.

After providing some time for students to read, Michael signals them that silent reading time is coming to an end. He states, "Please write a reflection about your reading in your reading log. Remember, if you would like to give a text talk to inspire others to read your text, this is a great time to plan what you would like to say."

Michael does just that. He prepares his text talk about the book he has been reading, *Giant Children* by Brod Bagert. He purposefully crafts his brief text talk by listing several of the hilarious topics in this poetry collection.

Once children are finished recording their reflections, Michael stands and invites others to give a text talk. When nobody volunteers, Michael declares, "I would like to pass on a text that I have been reading. It is hilarious and something that I think you might like." Michael walks over to the lidded basket that conceals the book he wants to share.

He begins, "Where can I find a poem or read about a turtle named Jaws?" He smiles, pauses, then slowly lifts the lid. He pulls out *Giant Children*, props it in front of the basket, and adds the title and author to the Pass It On! text chart.

Michael then turns to the students and plants a seed for a future text talk by thinking aloud, "I bet there is a great poem in there that you can talk about to pass it on to your classmates if you decide to read this book."

Text Suggestions

- *Barack Obama: Son of Promise, Child of Hope* by Nikki Grimes
- *Beetle McGrady Eats Bugs* by Megan McDonald
- *The Clever Stick* by John Lechner
- *Giant Children* by Brod Bagert
- *Muktar and the Camels* by Janet Graber
- *Willie and the All-Stars* by Floyd Cooper
- *Winning Words: Sports Stories and Photographs* by Charles R. Smith Jr.

Extension Ideas

★ Since the purpose behind the text talk is to broaden student exposure to a variety of gripping texts and to pass the texts on to others by talking about them, have students think of unusual and creative ways to do that. You may want to encourage students to write a one-minute commercial for their book. They are most likely well versed in the features and goals of commercials. Model a short commercial using a book like *Muktar and the Camels* by Janet Graber, reminding students not to give away the ending.

★ Show the class a YouTube clip of Siskel and Ebert or other professional movie critics reviewing a popular movie such as *Toy Story* or you can just talk to them about the concept of reviewers, people who watch a movie and tell you if they think you should see it. Tell them that they will get to be a reviewer for a book and share their opinions with the class. Ask them to write down their main points about why they thought it was a good book, and let them sit in a special "reviewer's chair" when they present. Consider encouraging different points of view by having two reviewers with different opinions of the book do a review, in true movie critic style.

SCENE-SATIONAL

Description: Many readers are drawn to a particular text because of the vivid characters in the story. Readers root for certain characters and clench their fists and teeth at others. They study some in an attempt to unravel their roles as the story unfolds. In other words, they often relate to the characters they encounter while reading. Readers sometimes even see themselves as one of the characters.

> ### Relating to Characters
>
> *Developing readers' awareness of story characters enables readers to relate to characters and fosters interest and understanding of what they are reading.*

Scene-sational enables striving readers to take a critical look at how the characters in a story inspire their interest. In small groups, striving readers articulate their views of the characters. Each group member chooses an interesting scene from the story to study a character more closely. He or she then memorizes the speech of the character and practices that character's behaviors.

Teaching Suggestions

1. Share your thinking about some of your favorite and least favorite characters and ask the students to share some of their favorite and least favorite characters as they turn-talk-and-listen with a neighbor.

2. As students talk, listen for interesting points that can be briefly shared with the whole class.

3. Inform the students that the purpose of this activity is to develop their

---

Scene-sational Procedures

1. Choose a character and examine one of the character's scenes. Several questions can be used to guide the examination.

   - Why do you like/dislike this character?
   - How would you describe the character?
   - What are the mannerisms of the character?
   - Why have you chosen this scene to share?

2. Talk about your character and scene with other students who are focusing on the same story.

3. Rehearse the scene that you will be acting out.

4. Act out your scene. Be sure to mimic the nonverbal behaviors and speech of the character in the scene you have chosen.

---

understanding of story characters in order to help them better comprehend the stories that they read.

4. Tell students that they will get to choose a story that they find fascinating because of the characters. It may be a book that they have already read or one they are reading currently.

5. Direct students to the chart that lists the Scene-sational procedures.

6. Allow students time to rehearse their scenes.

7. Invite individual students to act out their scene and lead a brief discussion with the whole class about their actions and the reasoning behind them.

Peering into the Classroom

Roland's third graders are seated at their desks waiting for the beginning of readers' workshop.

Roland begins his mini-lesson holding *Whopper Cake* by Karma Wilson and Will Hillenbrand, thumbing through the book and thinking aloud. "I just love this character! He is one of my favorites because he is so flashy and he comes up with crazy ideas." Turning his attention to his students, Roland comments, "Think about the characters of stories that you feel strongly about. Please use turn-talk-and-listen to share some

Readers' Workshop

Readers' workshop provides the scaffolded structure of a powerful reading lesson. Beginning with a brief mini-lesson, the teacher reviews or introduces a reading strategy or skill by modeling it.

Lesson Plans

Lesson plans are critical because they allow the teacher to set and articulate the purpose, change procedures when necessary, utilize supportive teaching aids, and differentiate instruction for individual students.

of your favorite or least favorite characters with a neighbor." His students immediately turn to face the person next to them at their desk groups. Their excitement for sharing their views of story characters is evident by their animated talking.

While students talk, Roland floats about the room making anecdotal notes to remind him of what he sees.

After several minutes, he brings the class back together by asking them if they have anything to share with the whole class. After a few people share, Roland points out to students the value of characterization in their lives as readers. He states, "You all speak so enthusiastically about these characters! I know that the characters help to make these some of your favorite stories. Learning more about characterization helps you to understand a story better." He holds up *Whopper Cake*, commenting, "I am going to show you an example of how you might develop and showcase your understanding of a character in an interesting story."

Roland continues, "This is one of my favorite scenes in the story." He sets down the book and begins to act it out. With one hand on his hip, he scratches his shaking head. A puzzled expression is painted across his face. Looking down at an imaginary bowl on the table, he mutters, in an old, crackly voice, "This bowl won't do."

In an instant, his face lights up. His eyes widen and his mouth gapes open. He snaps the fingers of the hand that was scratching his head. SNAP! "Eureka!" He shouts the next part of the character's line. "I have just the thing. We'll use the pickup bed!" He cranes his neck as if to peer out the window and states, "Go start that old jalopy, boys! And back it in real tight. Grandma's gonna be surprised when she gets home tonight!" He slaps his knee with excitement, earning snickers and the giggling amusement of his students. He then explains to students what they will do.

"You will get to play-act a favorite story of your own. The purpose is to strengthen your understanding of story characters by becoming one of the characters. You need to begin by thinking of a character that you have recently or are currently reading about. Be sure that you feel strongly about the character you choose. The character must have a speaking part in the story. Follow the steps on the Scene-sational Procedures chart to prepare."

Roland continues, "You will each get to act out your scenes over the next few days during readers' workshop. Your scene presentation may be similar to my model of Grandpa in *Whopper Cake*. Be sure to use your understanding of the character by speaking the character's lines and acting out their mannerisms while you rehearse." Roland closes the lesson by reminding students that examining and talking about story characters is an excellent way to better their understanding of what they have read. He encourages them to be on the lookout for interesting characters during their independent reading time and when reading at home.

Text Suggestions

- *Bobby Bramble Loses His Brain* by Dave Keane
- *Crazy Hair* by Neil Gaiman
- *In Our Mothers' House* by Patricia Polacco
- *The King's Taster* by Kenneth Oppel
- *Little Oink* by Amy Krouse Rosenthal
- *Lousy Rotten Stinkin' Grapes* by Margie Palatini
- *Whopper Cake* by Karma Wilson and Will Hillenbrand

Extension Ideas

★ Since characters are integral to a story, understanding who they are and why they do what they do is important to developing readers. One way students can have fun with characterization is to participate in a talk show format while in character. Students can choose to be different characters from one book, or perhaps from a series. For instance, *Little Oink* by Amy Krause Rosenthal is a book about a pig who wants to be clean. Students could choose to be Little Oink, Mama, Papa, one of his pals, or the talk show host. They could practice their answers to questions the talk show host will ask, speaking as the character. The talk show host could read the book aloud to the observers, giving them the background knowledge they would need to appreciate the character's answers. This format could also be used with well-known characters from different books, all answering generic questions from their character's point of view.

★ To further explore the concept of characters, consider using a book such as *Lousy Rotten Stinkin' Grapes* by Margie Palatini. This book is about a fox that hatches a scheme to get to some grapes hanging overhead. He refuses to listen to the suggestions of many different animals, saying he is the clever one. The characters could step up and give their versions of the story. Another fitting book is *The Dunderheads* by Paul Fleischman, a Roald Dahl–like book that features a diverse group of characters that all come together to accomplish one task. The story could be told through the voices of several characters.

YOU ARE THE TEXT

Description: Helping readers acquire academic language gives them greater understanding when reading subject-related texts. Freeman and Freeman (2007) make clear that there are three types of academic language. First, general academic language includes language that can be applied to all content areas. For instance, the terms *introduction* and *vocabulary* are integral parts of all subject-area texts. Second, content-specific terms like *connection* and *visualization*, which are associated with reading, are important for striving readers in order to assimilate and accommodate new information as they read and talk about reading. Finally, signal words like *however* and *furthermore* are those words that tie textual ideas together. Command of these three types of academic language allows striving readers to follow an author's line of thinking and understand contrasting and supporting information during readings and the discussions that follow.

You Are the Text calls on striving readers to have literature discussions without their texts. It provides opportunities for students to use academic language in authentic contexts. Students rely on their background knowledge, newly acquired information from their reading, and familiarity with the language used in the classroom to engage in a discussion. Essentially, each student participates in the discussion by speaking about what is pertinent to them individually and listening to what is important to others.

Teaching Suggestions

1. Invite students to choose a text.
2. Arrange students in reading groups according to common text, topic, or author.
3. Ask each group of students to collaboratively determine the amount of text they are to read for the first section and the time frame for the reading.
4. Inform the students that they will meet with their discussion groups without their texts.
5. Explain to students that coming together to discuss a text without the text in hand allows them to share their views, connections, and reactions to the reading.

Impress upon them that they are the text, that they bring meaning to what they are reading through personal experiences and background knowledge. The academic language that they use will showcase its relevance to them and their command of the strategies and terms that they use to make sense of the text.

6. Provide opportunities for the students to read their texts in class during silent reading and invite them to read at home as well.

7. On designated days, invite each group to discuss their books without their texts. If necessary, guide them to talk about discussion etiquette.

> ### Teacher Role
>
> *Since the purpose of this activity is to develop student command of academic language through practice, the teacher takes on the role of observer and listener to conduct formative assessments.*

Peering into the Classroom

Ryer invites his third graders to choose among eight texts for their literature discussions. Throughout the day, each student peruses the eight texts during individual work time or transitions to determine three texts that they would most like to read. They list the titles in order of preference and leave the lists on their desks when they depart at the end of the day. Ryer collects the lists and groups students according to their top choices and the number of texts available. He then makes a chart that shows these groups and places it in the front of the room for all to see. The following day, students examine the list and meet with their group members to plan their readings and schedule their discussions.

Terri, Jonas, Suzy, Jasmine, and Claire share their excitement with one another at getting the opportunity to read their first choice, *Most Loved in All the World* (Hegamin, 2009). Eager to begin reading, they collectively determine to read the entire book and discuss it the following day. Within minutes, they scatter to bean bags, desks, and comfy corners of the room to begin reading. Each responds differently while reading. Some choose to create a representative artifact to make greater sense during reading. Others create a story map to recall important story elements.

Terri creates a story map to illustrate the major events. Suzy simply reads and rereads the story. Jonas searches for other texts that remind him of the storyline. He gathers *Harriet Tubman, Mr. Lincoln's Way,* and *Henry's Freedom Box* as text-to-text connections.

On the day of their discussion, Terri, Jonas, Suzy, Jasmine, and Claire tuck themselves in a corner of their third-grade classroom. Having read the whole book during silent reading in class and later at home, they are now prepared to share their personal reactions *without* the book. Instead, "they are the text."

Jonas opens the discussion, stating, "I made several connections to other books we have read. Remember when Mr. Schendel read *Harriet Tubman* aloud?" Jonas asks. "And we all read *Henry's Freedom Box*."

"Hey, you're right," declares Terri. "Both are about slavery."

"Not only that, but they are about freedom, getting to freedom." Jonas adds. "Characters in both books try to free other slaves."

Jasmine adds, "Is that what *Henry's Freedom Box* was about, Jonas? Didn't Henry free himself?" she questions.

"He freed himself by mailing himself," Jonas says, nodding. "Yep."

Suzy digs deeper into the stories. "It must have been scary for Henry to ship himself, trapped in that box. And, just imagine how hard it was for the little girl's mom to send her away." Her face is scrunched up in sadness. "I can't even imagine having to do that."

"Yeah, I would be scared in the box and in the forest. Just visualize walking through a dark forest with someone you didn't even know. She was just a little girl. How old was she anyway, five?" Claire questions.

"Well, remember what Henry saw in town? His family was taken away from him," Terri remarks. "They did amazing things because they were treated so badly. The little girl's mom always came back from the master's house bleeding from whip marks!"

Ryer eavesdrops on the literature discussions, all the while taking anecdotal notes about how students use academic language. As the time comes to an end for this portion of readers' workshop, Ryer addresses the class again as a whole group. He says, "I saw many examples of you using school words related to reading. I noticed several of you using the word *connections* to describe other texts and experiences you remembered while reading. I heard a few of you making inferences and using the vocabulary in your texts to support your thinking. Also, you were describing the experiences of the characters using content-specific words like *slavery* and *freedom*." Ryer closes this readers' workshop with a reminder to students, "You can use terms that readers use to explain your understanding of what you are reading to others."

Text Suggestions

- *Big George: How a Shy Boy Became President Washington* by Anne Rockwell
- *The Butterfly* by Patricia Polacco
- *First Come the Zebra* by Lynne Barasch
- *The Greatest Story Never Told* by Ray Negron
- *I and I* by Tony Medina

- *Most Loved in All the World* by Tonya Cherie Hegamin
- *Star of the Week* by Darlene Friedman

Extension Ideas

★ Another way for students to practice using academic language is to encourage them to be metacognitive about the language they are using in discussions. Holding up little signs indicating the type of language they are using in their comments makes their metacognition more tangible. A paper with premade signs on it could be passed out to each student, and students could cut out their signs quickly and attach them to a Popsicle stick. The signs could say "general language," "content specific" and "signal words." As they speak, ask students to quickly hold up a sign if they are using any of these types of language in their comments. Give them practice before their discussion by using academic language in sentences and having them hold up the signs.

★ The point of You Are the Text is to allow students to share their views, connections, and reactions to the reading. Have students choose a book like *First Come the Zebra* by Lynne Barasch and read it silently. When they are finished, encourage them to think about the connections they can make to the text, the reactions they have to it, and their views about the book or the questions it raises. During the small-group discussion, encourage them to start their sentences with phrases that indicate how they are connecting to the text, saying things like "The connection I made to the text . . ." or "My reaction to the ending was . . . ."

RESTORY TELLER

Description: There are many reasons to use story retelling to support readers. Story retelling improves oral language skills, enhances story comprehension, heightens a sense of story structure, and improves the command of structural elements in writing. Furthermore, story retelling can be used to nurture community by allowing students to share interesting tales depicting their own lives or cultural backgrounds.

ReStory Teller is one way for striving readers to strengthen their command of story structure and improve reading comprehension. It gives students a structure for talking about story sense and retelling familiar stories. Through practice, striving readers take ownership of a story by telling it to others. As peers and their teacher discuss story elements (e.g., characters, setting, problem, events, details, solution), they breathe life into the story.

Teaching Suggestions

1. Explicitly state that the purpose of this activity is to gain a greater understanding of story elements and structure by becoming thoroughly familiar with a story.

2. Invite students to select a story that is of interest and is appropriate for their classroom audience.

3. Provide time for students to read, study, and map the key elements of their stories.

4. Encourage students to identify and memorize key phrases or parts but not the entire story.

5. As they prepare, stress the importance of speaking with expression and emotion to bring the story to life.

6. Remind students of the importance of looking directly at the audience when speaking. Doing so helps everyone feel more involved in the story.

7. Provide time for students to practice rereading the story and rehearsing for the performance.

Peering into the Classroom

Lindsey tells her fourth-grade students, "Think of a person who is a great storyteller. What makes his or her storytelling so great?"

Zack offers, "My mom used to tell amazing bedtime stories when I was a little kid. She would describe the settings so well that I could see them. I remember feeling like I was there, in the stories!"

"My Papa tells awesome stories," says Dominique. With large, round eyes, he adds, "His characters are very interesting and I hope for them as they try to solve problems."

"Excellent examples, you two!" Lindsey comments. "You have given us clear examples of the value of telling stories to others. In order to tell a powerful story, the storyteller must know the main parts of a story and include those elements in their oral tales. Knowing those story elements also makes you a better reader by helping you to follow the story's direction."

Lindsey continues, "You will get the opportunity to become storytellers. To start, you get to read a story that you find interesting. After studying the story, you will tell the tale to the class through a "ReStory." The purpose is for you to use talking to learn more about the story elements like setting, characterization, events, problem, and solution that we have been studying in connection with the stories I have been reading aloud to you."

Lindsey asks her students to locate a text for the activity. As she watches students select texts of interest, her attention falls on Dominique, a striving reader. He has had difficulty locating texts of interest in the past. This time, with an explicit purpose in mind, Dominique rushes over to the classroom library and chooses a favorite, familiar text, the retold fairy tale *Hansel and Gretel* by Rachel Isadora.

Dominique reads and rereads the text several times over the next few days during the silent reading portion of readers' workshop. Familiar with story mapping, he applies his drawing skills as he recreates the characters, the setting, and all of the main events that he plans to include in his "restory."

"Be sure to speak with expression and the appropriate emotion just like your Papa does when he tells a story. That will make it more interesting for your audience," explains Lindsey. "It will also make everyone more involved if you look at them while you tell your story," she adds.

"Keep practicing and let me know when you are ready to perform, Dominique. I will schedule it at the beginning of readers' workshop as the mini-lesson model for the rest of the class." Lindsey continues to conference with students. The following day she provides time for students to perform.

Text Suggestions

- *Boy Dumplings* by Ying Chang Compestine
- *Cool Cat* by Nonny Hogrogian
- *Finn Throws a Fit* by David Elliott
- *The Gigantic Turnip* by Aleksei Tolstoy
- *Hansel and Gretel* by Rachel Isadora
- *Molly Who Flew Away* by Valeri Gorbachev
- *The Ugly Duckling* by Rachel Isadora

Extension Ideas

★ Another way to practice retelling a story to work on reading comprehension is to have students take on the role of a news reporter, delivering the key parts of the story with expression and a sense of purpose. Props like an overcoat and a microphone add authenticity and interest. Help students pick books that lend themselves to this type of retelling, such as *Finn Throws a Fit* by David Elliott.

★ Incorporating audience participation into a story retelling is a variation of ReStory Teller. Using a book with a fairly simple storyline and characters is best. For example, *The Gigantic Turnip* by Aleksei Tolstoy has two main characters, an old man and an old woman. They have six canaries, five white geese, four speckled hens, three black cats, two pot-bellied pigs, one brown cow, and also one mouse. The reader's job is to act as the narrator while the other students act as supporting characters. The characters have simple actions, making it easier to manage, and the narrator's job is to keep the story flowing while the characters act it out.

LISTENING
SPEAKING
CHAPTER 4
VIEWING
WRITING
READING

Reading Strategies

How do children learn to read? Why do some find reading difficult? What are some effective ways of helping children who find learning to read difficult? Answers to these important questions are grounded in one's beliefs. We believe that learning to read comes from an abundance of purposeful, meaningful reading practice. We advocate using a variety of assessment techniques to discover what students know and need to know to help guide them toward becoming motivated, lifelong readers. These discoveries lead to targeted, explicit instruction that capitalizes on students' strengths. The teaching strategies we offer in this chapter magnify the importance of providing students with a lot of reading practice within the school day. We propose five good reasons for using authentic reading experiences to support the development of striving readers.

★ *Immersion in texts and the other language arts fosters concept knowledge understanding.* Reading about particular topics from a variety of sources allows striving readers to add to understandings they acquire through listening, speaking, and viewing. Furthermore, nurturing the other language arts such as listening and speaking during discussions allows striving readers to make connections among them.

Reading Skills	Paired Reading	Buddy Reading	Focused Readers' Workshop	Cut Apart	Text Slam
reading interest	●	●	●	●	●
seeing text as accessible	●	●	●	●	●
fluency	●	●	●	●	●
predicting		●	●		
summarizing	●		●		
connecting			●	●	
questioning		●	●		
synthesizing			●		
inferring			●		
visualizing		●	●		●
monitoring comprehension	●	●	●	●	●
determining importance		●	●		●
listening comprehension	●		●	●	●
gathering facts			●		
social vocabulary		●	●		
academic vocabulary		●	●		
sequence of events			●	●	

Figure 4.1. Reading teaching strategies and the reading skills they nurture

★ *25 Essential Language Arts Strategies to Help Striving Readers Succeed*

- ★ *Practice makes perfect.* Reading makes better readers. Given explicit reading instruction along with plenty of time to read independently, readers get the opportunity to apply and practice reading skills and to enjoy reading.

- ★ *Reading becomes habitual.* Perpetuating a behavior builds stamina. Avid readers emerge from regularly scheduled opportunities to read for individual purposes.

- ★ *Reading becomes an accessible task.* Allowing readers time to read texts of interest nurtures their joy of reading. This positive mind-set toward reading makes reading assigned texts with understanding and interest more plausible.

- ★ *Striving readers acquire a greater understanding of what it means to be a reader.* Experience in reading allows striving readers to assimilate and accommodate new information about the process for reading and what is read. Readers build their reading schema when they are given abundant opportunities to read with purpose.

With these reasons in mind, we showcase five ways to use reading to enhance reading ability. Figure 4.1 shows these teaching strategies and the skills they elicit.

PAIRED READING

Description: Providing a model of how reading should sound and offering explicit examples of self-monitoring behaviors enable developing readers to view skillful reading. Beyond modeling, one-on-one tutorials offer continued guidance and support to developing readers while practicing reading.

Paired Reading is one way to make the reading process explicit and to guide the reading practice of striving readers. A striving reader is paired with a more experienced reader (e.g., teacher, parent volunteer, student from a higher grade) who provides appropriate support and assistance. The reading sessions begin with choral reading from a text chosen by and of interest to the striving reader. As the reading ensues, the experienced reader encourages the striving reader to self-monitor.

> ### Volunteer Tutors
>
> *If volunteers serve as tutors, provide an overview of the purpose and procedure for conducting paired reading. Invite volunteers to observe a teacher-modeled paired reading session or two to learn the process.*

Teaching Suggestions

1. Determine a schedule for meeting with striving readers.
2. Share the purpose of the paired reading with individual striving readers—to help them better understand what good reading sounds, looks, and feels like (all the while focused on meaning) and to emulate each through plenty of reading practice.
3. Request that the striving reader bring a text of interest to the paired reading session.
4. Establish a signal that indicates when the reader would like to read aloud on their own. The signal may be a tap on the tutor's arm or a nod of the reader's head.
5. Begin by reading aloud together on the reader's cue.
6. Attend to student reading behaviors and take advantage of stopping points to discuss the meaning of the text.
7. Focus on all miscues made by the reader. If the reader does not self-correct a miscue, point to the word and ask the appropriate cueing question.
8. If the miscue changes the meaning of the text, ask, "Does that make sense?"
9. If the miscue changes the structure or sound of the text, ask, "Does that sound right?"
10. If the miscue changes the image of the text, ask, "Does that look right?
11. Provide time for the student to correct the miscue based on the prompt

---

Types of Reading Miscues

- *Semantic Miscue.* A semantic miscue results when a word is changed, modifying the meaning of the text. Omitting a word may result in a change of text meaning.

- *Syntax Miscue.* A syntax miscue results when the text structure or grammar is changed. Substituting verb tense and reading *run* in place of *ran* changes the sound of the text.

- *Graphophonic Miscue.* A graphophonic miscue results when a word is slightly modified. Reading the word *house* instead of *home* is an example.

given. Tell the student the correct word if they require additional support.

12. Resume the reading together until the signal is given for solo reading. Continue attending to student self-monitoring and offer support as needed.

Peering into the Classroom

Veronica decides to use Paired Reading to work one on one with her second-grade striving readers to guide their self-monitoring skills while reading interesting texts. At the beginning of silent reading, she tells her second graders, "I know how much you love reading the books you choose during silent reading." She adds, "You do a beautiful job of practicing reading and you are becoming excellent readers! I would like to help you become even better readers. During our silent reading portion of readers' workshop today, I will begin "paired reading" with some students. I will invite one of you to join me so that we can read together. Since we will be reading aloud and do not want to disrupt others, we will read at the back of the room." She pauses, and then continues, "In order for you to understand your role and my expectations, I will walk you through the paired reading process using a fishbowl model."

Veronica asks the students to assemble themselves in a circle around the center island of desks. Once assembled, she positions herself at the center island and explains the purpose of paired reading. She states, "The purpose of paired reading is for you to practice reading a text with my support. I will provide support by modeling how fluent reading sounds. Not only that, I will pay attention to and guide your use of self-monitoring while you read to me. Self-monitoring is when you know you are not understanding something and you do something to correct yourself."

"Reading a book that really interests you is important. You may decide to bring several books, knowing that you can change your text at any time during our fifteen minutes together," Veronica explains.

Exchanging Texts

Reading enjoyment is enhanced when students realize that it is okay to abandon a book that doesn't hold their interest.

Fishbowl Modeling

The "fishbowl" method allows a small group of students to model the use of an academic skill or a classroom activity for their peers who are gathered in a circle around them. A reflective discussion from the audience and members of the fishbowl group follows the fishbowl.

"We will always begin by reading aloud together while one of us points to the words. This will allow us to match each word being read with its print. We also need to determine a signal that allows readers to indicate that they would like to continue reading aloud on their own. How about a tap on my arm? Does that sound good?" The students nod in agreement.

"We are about ready to begin. Again, we will begin reading together and when you want to read alone, you tap my arm. I will then be quiet and you will continue reading while I watch and listen. Any time that you read a word differently than what is written in the text you should use your reading strategies to correct yourself. If you do not self-correct, I will point to the word and ask you a question about the miscue to help you practice what great readers do while they read. If you need help figuring out your mistake, I will help you. Then we will start reading aloud together again. You will signal me when you are ready to continue reading on your own." Veronica continues, "Oh, there is one more thing. I will stop you once in a while to discuss the meaning of what you have just read."

Veronica tells the group, "Genessee and I will model the process for you." With that, Veronica and Genessee demonstrate paired reading. Students then return to their desks, bean bags, and comfy reading nooks to begin silent reading and practice self-monitoring while Veronica invites a striving reader to join her for paired reading.

Text Suggestions

- *Big Nate: In a Class by Himself* by Lincoln Peirce
- *Caterpillar, Caterpillar* by Vivian French
- *The Frog Scientist* by Pamela S. Turner
- *The Girls' Book of Excellence* by Sally Norton
- *Probuditi!* by Chris Van Allsburg
- *Stink-O-Pedia* by Megan McDonald
- *Your Backyard Is Wild!* by Jeff Corwin

Extension Ideas

★ After students are familiar with the routine of paired reading, consider asking them if they'd like to turn the tables and be the expert in the pair. Explain that they will be following the same procedure as described, but the adult (or experienced reader) will be the reader, and the striving reader will act as the guiding partner. The "reader" will intentionally miscue, sometimes self-correcting, sometimes not. The guiding partner will practice asking the appropriate cueing questions to help support the reader. A page containing the cueing questions could be provided for reference. Modeling this topsy-turvy way of paired reading using the fishbowl model would be important, as students would be looking at the activity from a much different perspective.

★ A variation of paired reading if a partner is not available is to use a book on tape. Explaining the purpose for using the book on tape is important, because it will be used in a different way for this activity. Explain and model the following process for the class.

1. Choose a book on tape that features oral reading at a rate the student can keep up with that is around the student's approximate reading level, such as *Caterpillar, Caterpillar* by Vivian French.

2. Prepare a copy of the text and make enough copies for each student. This is the individual's copy to mark on. Provide a highlighter marker as well.

3. Position the CD/tape player so that it can easily be paused.

4. Instruct students to listen to the book on tape once through, silently following along with the text.

5. The second time through, read aloud, along with the tape.

6. If there is a miscue, stop the tape and highlight it.

7. Stop the tape any time meaning breaks down and reread or use another strategy to insure understanding.

8. When the tape is over, review the miscues. Attempt to figure them out individually, but ask for assistance if needed.

9. Read along with the tape again, as desired.

BUDDY READING

Description: Readers need ample opportunities to read in order for them to draw from available reading strategies and apply appropriate skills that ensure reading success. To extend their understanding of reading, though, having students teach reading to one another is a surefire way to elevate their understanding. Teaching another also requires that the "teacher" use essential reading skills at a higher level. Buddy reading is a vehicle for this kind of teaching and learning. It also helps striving readers strengthen their confidence and skills.

Teaching Suggestions

1. Invite students to discuss what they know about learning to read. Ideas to highlight include:

    -   Learning that print carries meaning
    -   Learning that a book is arranged in a particular way
    -   Learning the joy associated with reading
    -   Learning the value of having time to read
    -   Learning that reading is purposeful
    -   Learning the skills associated with reading
    -   Learning that there are different types of text

2. Inform students that they will get an opportunity to share the reading process with younger students through a process called "buddy reading."

3. Share with students the purposes of buddy reading, noting that it will help them gain a greater understanding of how to apply their reading skills, will give them time to practice those skills during reading, and will help them to develop reading confidence. Buddy reading also will provide good models of effective reading.

4. Post the Buddy Reading Expectations chart in the classroom for future reference.

5. Remind students that they may initially choose to read aloud to simply enjoy a great text with little or no questioning. The main purpose is to ignite a passion for reading in their buddy reader.

6. Model the process or have the students role-play to establish a clear picture of buddy reading.

Peering into the Classroom

Ruth knows that her fourth-graders understand concepts and are able to develop a greater command of skills when they get the opportunity to teach others. Therefore, she decides to add "buddy reading" to the activities that are a regular part of her

Buddy Reading Expectations

1. Sit side by side.

2. Get your buddy excited about the text.

3. Let the younger reader hold the text.

4. Identify the author and illustrator before reading.

5. Take a picture walk, allowing your buddy to predict what the story/text will be about.

6. Read the text aloud with enthusiasm.

7. Talk about the text during the reading.
   - Use questioning (Why did . . . ?)
   - Think aloud (I wonder why . . . ?)
   - Make predictions (What do you think will happen?)
   - Make connections (This reminds me of . . . .)

8. Discuss the text during and after the reading.

classroom routines. She sets out to explore opportunities for starting a buddy reading program between her fourth graders and the kindergartners who attend her school. She approaches Janet, the kindergarten teacher, and Janet, too, thinks it is an excellent idea. Elated, Ruth begins to prepare her students.

Ruth asks her fourth-grade students, "What do you know about learning to read? I want you to turn-talk-and-listen to a neighbor to answer this question." The classroom erupts with paired conversations about their reading perceptions and experiences.

Matilda says to Lauryn, "I know that learning to read has been easy for me because I have always been around books. I have loved to read ever since I was a little girl."

Lauryn replies, "Reading has always been hard for me, but I still like it. The more I learn about ways to make sense of what the author is saying, the easier it gets. It's a lot easier when I like what I am reading about."

Recruiting Help in the Classroom

Solicit the help of other teachers, the literacy coach, speech therapist, and other specialists to monitor buddies during buddy reading. They can also offer instructional support when necessary.

Stanley tells Cindy, "I remember learning to read by memorizing books. Sooner or later I was able to actually read them.

"Yeah, I did the same thing," says Cindy. "I have learned to like reading more since I found interesting things to read like nonfiction books. I love to read because I can learn about things like horses and skiing."

After listening in on several students, Ruth addresses the class as a whole. "Wow, it sounds like you are reading experts! Now you're going to get the opportunity to share your reading knowledge and skills with others. You will be buddy reading with Mrs. Kozlowski's kindergarten students. Reading aloud to them will help you better understand and practice your reading skills. And all that practice will make you better readers. Your goal will be to model reading for your buddies and get them excited about becoming readers themselves!"

"Understanding what to do when you go to buddy reading is important," Ruth says, "so let's review the expectations for buddy reading and see just what it looks like."

She displays the poster that lists Buddy Reading Expectations and provides time for students to silently read through the list and ask for clarification as needed.

After several minutes, Kade asks, "How do we get them excited about reading?"

Ruth poses Kade's question to the rest of the class and Ryan is quick to share his idea.

"We act excited!" Ryan shares. Claire adds, "We can get them excited by choosing a book that they are interested in."

"Both of you are right," Ruth comments. "Now I want you to each choose a partner and pick a book that you think he or she will like. Then you will spread out around the room and practice buddy reading with each other. Just be sure to pretend that your buddy is a kindergartner. This will help you prepare for your actual kindergarten buddy. Your practice will also help you to use appropriate strategies and skills whenever you read."

Ruth's fourth graders pair up and choose their texts. They then act out their readings with animated voices and facial expressions. They continue to prepare over the next few days during the reading practice portion of readers' workshop.

Text Suggestions

- *A-B-C Discovery!* by Izhar Cohen
- *Clang! Clang! Beep! Beep! Listen to the City* by Robert Burleigh
- *Forever Friends* by Carin Berger
- *Hot Rod Hamster* by Cynthia Lord
- *Itty Bitty* by Cece Bell

- *The Odd Egg* by Emily Gravett
- *Snow! Snow! Snow!* by Lee Harper

Extension Ideas

★ Since students will be teaching reading to others, offering students a chance to think about what they specifically want their buddy to learn can take it a step further. Ask students to think about what three aspects of reading they want to highlight when working with their buddy. Tell them they are going to design a rubric to give to their buddy based on those three aspects after the buddy reading session is over. Model how to write a simple rubric, using a happy face, a solemn face, and a sad face for young buddies to use. The rubric should focus on the teaching of the concept through a specific book. Support them as they write their rubrics, and ask them to read their text with a partner in class, test-driving the rubric, making sure it matches the text and the concepts. They can then introduce it during buddy reading.

★ Students can think of one aspect they've learned about reading from working with their reading buddies and teach a mini-lesson based on that aspect to the class. They can use a book they used with their buddy to illustrate that aspect of reading and share their reflections on the experience with their classmates, celebrating all the different things they learned about reading through their work with their buddy.

FOCUSED READERS' WORKSHOP

Description: Focused Readers' Workshop (Opitz & Ford, 2008) provides the structure and opportunity for striving readers to take ownership of their reading growth. The personal and academic needs of readers are supported by their teacher's understanding of subject matter and the pedagogy of teaching reading. Following the belief that readers learn by reading, Focused Readers' Workshop is structured around an abundance of reading time.

The four-part workshop begins with a brief, teacher-directed lesson presented to the whole class. A specified silent reading time, allowing striving readers to choose from a teacher-provided group of texts (organized by genre, topic, theme, author, or literary element) at their desired pace follows. The third part, which may be intermingled with individual reading time, includes time for striving readers to respond to their readings. During silent reading and reading response, the teacher conferences with individuals or small groups to assess reading progress and provide further instruction as necessary. The readers' workshop concludes with student sharing in pairs or small groups followed by whole-class sharing and wrap-up.

Teaching Suggestions

1. Plan the teacher-directed mini-lesson, conferencing schedule, response activities for individuals, and the whole-group wrap-up activity according to student strengths, needs, and interests as identified by previous reading assessments.

> **Mentor Texts**
>
> *Sometimes teachers refer to texts used to model reading skills and strategies as mentor texts.*

2. Select texts according to a common element with varying levels of student ability and interest in mind. Display the texts in a clearly designated area of the classroom.

3. Invite students to choose a text from the collection provided. Instruct them to choose according to their interest and ability. Inform them that they must be able to read the text independently. Encourage some students to begin reading their texts while others continue to choose. This will allow students to determine their level of interest and whether they are able to read the text chosen independently. Allow students to exchange texts if necessary.

4. Share the purpose of the teacher-directed mini-lesson. For example, you may state, "This lesson is intended to help you identify examples of *simile* in texts and to explain their meaning. This understanding will allow you to use similes to make your own writing more descriptive and help you to understand the author's intended meaning."

5. Teach the mini-lesson. Read aloud a portion of text to model the task, reading skill, or comprehension strategy of interest.

6. Model how to do the activity, giving attention to the instructions displayed on the board. State the time allotted for each portion of the workshop.

7. Encourage students to ask questions for clarification.

8. Invite students to begin reading silently. Instruct them to follow the displayed instructions to record their responses. Conference with individuals and small groups to assess understanding and progress. Provide further instructional support as necessary.

9. Allow students to work in pairs or small groups for a specified amount of time

after the individual response period has ended. Encourage students to extend their understanding through discussion and sharing examples with peers.

10. Invite students to come together for whole-group sharing and the lesson wrap-up.

Peering into the Classroom

Carson's third graders have been learning how to make their writing more descriptive. He decides to enhance student understanding of descriptive writing by exploring the use of similes in authentic texts. Incorporating an exploration of similes into Focused Readers' Workshop will allow students to explore their use while they read. He knows that the instructional guidance and opportunities to learn through interaction with peers will support the success of his striving readers. He decides to model the identification of similes using read-aloud and think-aloud in a brief mini-lesson at the beginning of the workshop.

Attentive to the reading abilities and interests of students, striving readers included, Carson collects texts that include multiple examples of similes. He displays the texts for students to choose from on two tables at the front of the classroom.

"Readers' workshop is going to be a little different today. For our Focused Readers' Workshop, you will need to choose a text from one of these two tables," Carson says as he gestures to the tables covered with books. "Please choose a text that you are interested in, one that you are able to read independently from this group." He models the process by peering over the collection, picking up a picture book, studying its front and back covers, reading part of the inside jacket, thumbing through several pages, and reading a portion of a randomly chosen page silently. He places the text on his desk. "While others continue choosing a text, you are welcome to begin reading the one you have chosen to make sure it is of interest to you and you are able to read it by yourself."

As necessary, Carson assists students in choosing their texts. He guides several students to texts he has selected with them in mind, but allows them to make the final decision. The entire selection process takes only a few minutes even with several last-minute exchanges.

"We have been working on developing our descriptive writing. We are now going to search for examples of descriptive writing in texts. This is a 'Simile Scavenger Hunt.' You are familiar with similes as a result of yesterday's poetry read-aloud and discussion. The purpose of this lesson is to help you identify examples of similes in texts and to explain their meanings. This will help you to begin using similes to make your own writing more descriptive."

Carson begins the lesson by stating, "I am going to model the steps of the process for identifying and exploring the meaning of similes with this text." He holds up *Sea Horse: The Shyest Fish in the Sea* by Chris Butterworth, the previously selected picture book. He reads aloud until he finds a simile. "Hey, there is a simile!" he exclaims. "The text says that a creature with 'an eye like a small black bead' is watching from the sea-grass. I can picture that eye because I know what a small black bead looks like." Carson thinks aloud and turns to a two-column chart he has created. On the top of the left-hand column he writes *Simile*. On the top of the right-hand column he writes *Meaning*. He writes *eye like a small black bead* in the left-hand column and *tiny black dot* in the right-hand column. Carson continues reading several more pages to locate more examples of simile and follows the same process for recording them.

After locating three similes, Carson says, "This is the process you will use as you read and search for similes in the texts you have chosen." Pointing to the simile chart, he states, "I have created this Simile Scavenger Hunt Procedures chart to remind you of what you need to do today."

Students create their two-column charts and begin reading their texts. Carson begins conferencing with individual readers and those students he suspects may need support identifying similes. He checks to see that the student can read the text, identify a simile, and determine its meaning. He also checks to be sure that the student can follow the format for recording the information. He offers support as necessary and moves on to conference with others.

Simile Scavenger Hunt Procedures

1. Create a two-column chart in your reading log. Title each column.
2. Read your book silently.
3. Identify as many similes as possible from your text.
4. Record each simile and its meaning on your two-column chart.
5. Continue reading and searching for similes until you get the signal to share with a partner.
6. Taking turns, share your similes and meanings with your partner.
7. Discuss the meanings of your similes, referring to your texts for support. Make changes to meanings if necessary.

Approximately 20 minutes later, Carson signals readers to stop collecting similes and to choose a neighbor for turn-talk-and-listen. He instructs them to continue following procedural steps 6 and 7. He goes from pair to pair, assessing student collaboration and understanding by listening in on their conversations. After five minutes, Carson brings the class together for the wrap-up. Once volunteers have shared some similes, he closes the lesson, stating, "So remember, searching for literary elements like similes and considering their meanings is one way to determine what the author is describing. Understanding them will help you to comprehend."

Text Suggestions

- *Bunion Burt* by Marsha Hayles
- *Everybody Was a Baby Once* by Allan Ahlberg
- *I Love You So . . .* by Marianne Richmond
- *My Mom* by Anthony Browne
- *Not a Stick* by Antoinette Portis
- *Sea Horse: The Shyest Fish in the Sea* by Chris Butterworth
- *Smile!* by Leigh Hodgkinson

Extension Ideas

★ One advantage of Focused Readers' Workshop is that it can be adapted to the needs of the classroom and can focus on a literary element, a text feature, a strategy or skill, a theme, an author, a genre, or a topic. It can be teacher- or student-driven, but it comes from student interest, strength, or need. Exploring typographical features is an example of one such focus. Gather a collection of books that feature words written in unusual ways that produce visual interest— bold, italicized, wrapping around pictures, typed vertically, written to reflect the meaning of the word, etc. Read *Smile!* aloud as a mentor text, using your voice to reflect the differences in the typographic features. Ask students to listen for these differences, showing the text to them as you read. Ask them how they might know to read a word differently, leading them to notice the typographical features. Tell them that during the focused readers' workshop, they will be looking for how the author uses typographical features to create interest visually and to cue oral reading. Provide them with a plain piece of paper, and allow them to choose books from the collection. Instruct them to find words from the book that are written in an unusual way and to write them down on their paper exactly as they are written in the book, reflecting on why they are written that way. Once they've found several, invite them to pick their favorite three to write on a classroom word mural. If desired, students can share the words they put on the mural, the context of the words in the sentence/paragraph, and why they believe the author chose to write them the way that he or she did.

★ Focusing the workshop on a topic is an excellent way to help students contribute to one another's learning, regardless of reading level. For example, all students might read about robots. All would read "just-right" texts and report discoveries they glean from their texts with the whole class.

CUT APART

Description: Developing oral reading fluency requires attention to appropriate pace, accuracy, and expression (Opitz, 2007). Fluent readers can show their understanding of text structure and comprehension of content by varying reading pace, and attending to commas and periods makes reading a story aloud sound natural. Reading accuracy requires opportunities for readers to practice reading and rereading a story so that they can become familiar with it. They can then read the text aloud with confidence and precision. As Erekson (2010) reminds us, readers bring a text to life through inflection, stress, tempo, and phrasing.

Cut Apart is one way to teach fluency to striving readers. A text is cut apart into enough sections so that each student in the class has a part to read. As striving readers practice and become more familiar with their portion of text, they gain reading confidence. In essence, using Cut Apart enables striving readers to read and listen to stories with enhanced comprehension.

Teaching Suggestions

1. Identify a text appropriate for the reading ability of students.
2. Photocopy the text, adjusting the size of the print as necessary.
3. Read through the text, identifying logical stopping points to determine section to be read by individual students.
4. Cut the photocopied text apart. Paste each section on a note card and number the cards in the order the sections appear in the story.
5. Inform students that a story has been cut apart so that each of them has a part to read.

Cut Apart Procedures

1. Practice reading your part silently.

2. After reading your part the first time, think about how you will read it aloud to the class. Think about these questions as you prepare:
   - What parts should be read more slowly?
   - What parts should be read more quickly?
   - Am I reading each word accurately?
   - How can I read my part with expression?
   - What do I want readers to understand?

3. Continue your reading practice until it is time to share.

6. Explain the purpose of the activity—to help all students develop oral reading fluency and listening comprehension skills. Students will practice reading a text silently to determine an appropriate reading pace. They will make sure to read words accurately and with expression.

7. Explain the expectations for the activity by referring to the Cut Apart Procedures chart displayed at the front of the classroom.

8. Hand out the cards, inviting students to begin following the procedures. Sections of text may be handed out randomly or matched with individuals purposefully according to reading ability. Circulate the room attending to individual striving readers, providing assistance as necessary.

9. Gather students in a large circle in numerical order according to the number on each card. Ask students to leave their cards facedown until it is their turn to read. Guide students to focus on what is happening in the story and how fluency helps to enhance it.

10. Begin by reading the title, author, and illustrator yourself. Have the students follow in turn according to their numbered cards.

Peering into the Classroom

Believing that reading fluency pertains to appropriate pacing, accuracy, and expression, Brian prepares a Cut Apart activity for his second graders to practice all three. He decides to use the poetic story *Our Marching Band* by Lloyd Moss because the stanzas will allow natural portions of text to be divided among students. Not only that, the poetic text will allow students essential practice varying reading pace and reading with expression. Brian copies the text, numbers each section before cutting them apart, and pastes them on individual 3 by 5 note cards.

The next day Brian tells his second graders, "Today we are going to read a story in a different way. I have cut apart the story and put each part on a note card," says Brian, holding up the cards. He continues, "You will each get a card to read. The number on the card will tell you where your part fits in the story. The purpose of this activity is to help you develop oral reading fluency and listening comprehension. You will practice reading your portion of text silently to prepare for reading it aloud to the class. You will know what to do by following the procedures listed here on this chart," says Brian, pointing to the Cut Apart Procedures poster he created earlier. "While you silently read, I want you to ask yourself these four questions." He points to the questions listed on the poster and asks his students to study them for a moment. "What questions might you have?"

"What do you mean by reading more slowly and quickly?" Harvey asks.

"Reading more slowly and quickly has to do with your reading pace," Brian clarifies.

Hannah asks, "Is that like when you read aloud to us? When the story gets more interesting and something exciting is happening you start to read faster."

"Yes, Hannah, that's it!" Brian states, adding, "I read faster because the story is getting more interesting. It is natural to read more quickly in anticipation of what will happen next in the story. Good readers also read more slowly when they come to parts that are descriptive. Pausing between details that are used to describe the setting or something a character says or does helps the reader make sense of the story and follow along. Varying reading pace allows a reader to show his or her understanding of the story and also allows listeners to understand the story as it is read aloud."

"What do you know about reading with expression?" Brian inquires.

"Well, we read with expression when we pay attention to exclamation marks when reading to our buddy readers," shares Steven. "We read those sentences with excitement."

"That is an excellent example!" Brian exclaims.

"You just *spoke* with expression right there!" Susan adds.

"So did you, Susan," Brian responds, smiling.

"Now, before we begin, I would like you to turn-talk-and-listen with your neighbor to go over the steps of the procedures," says Brian. He then walks around the classroom, listening in on student conversations to check for understanding. "Great, it sounds like you know just what to do. When you get your card, I want you to start reading silently and follow the steps on the poster," explains Brian as he hands out the cards. "As you practice, I will be coming around to help if necessary. Please begin."

Excitedly, students begin reading silently. Brian circulates among the students, checking in on striving readers he suspects may need support. He asks them to read aloud and listens to determine that the student can read the text accurately and identify possible variations of pace and expression. Brian also checks that the student understands what is being read. He offers support as necessary and moves on to check on others.

After several minutes, Brian gathers students in a large circle according to the number written on their cards. He explains and models what he expects them to do as they listen to others reading. He then begins by reading his own card, which lists the title, author, and illustrator. Students read aloud in turn. Brian closes the lesson by reminding students, "Reading with understanding is something that helps you decide the appropriate pace for reading to others and how to use your voice so that you can bring the story to life when sharing it with others."

Text Suggestions

- *Hotel Deep* by Kurt Cyrus
- *The Looking Book* by Mary Ann Hoberman
- *¡Marimba! Animales From A to Z* by Pat Mora
- *One Fine Trade* by Bobbi Miller
- *Our Marching Band* by Lloyd Moss
- *Poison!* by Tammi Salzano
- *Silly Street* by Jeff Foxworthy

Extension Ideas

★ Use a book such as *Hotel Deep* by Kurt Cyrus to extend a Cut Apart session. Go through the steps of the activity, assigning each student a part. Allow students time to practice and then to read each part in turn. Collect the cards, and show posters that have the same text from *Hotel Deep* written on them. Randomly assign students to groups of four, and give each group a different poster. Allow time for each group to practice reading. Explain the procedures for reading the posters in turn, and do the choral reading. Then tell each group they need to illustrate their part of the story using art supplies. Provide students time to create. Have groups add their illustration to the hotel in turn, reading their part as they do so.

 Have students go through another Cut Apart session as described above, but with the purpose of performing it for another classroom, perhaps the one their reading buddies are from. A hilarious book like *The Big Fat Cow That Goes Kapow* by Andy Griffiths would work well for this, with pairs or trios choosing one of the ten story poems from the book to perform. Have different students explain the purpose of each step of the Cut Apart to the class they are performing for, focusing on things like reading pace, experiencing a story emotionally, and reading with accuracy, confidence, and expression.

★ ★ ★

TEXT SLAM

Description: Text Slam is one way to ignite a burning desire to read in striving readers. This activity relies heavily on student interest. Readers are invited to choose *any* appropriate text that is of personal interest (e.g., poetry, narratives, informational, song texts). Readers choose an entire text or a portion to be read aloud to their classroom audience. The teacher allots time for students to practice during the school day.

Teaching Suggestions

1. Explain the purpose of Text Slam to students—to identify captivating texts and make reading fun. Students develop a greater understanding of reading fluency by preparing and performing a read-aloud for others.

2. Tell students that they will get to choose a text that they are passionate about. The text may be from another author or one of their own creations.

3. Inform students that they will be reading the text without props or musical support so they will need to consider how their voices and nonverbal actions will enhance the performance.

4. Encourage students to identify a compelling portion of the text to read for others.

5. Invite students to focus on an emotion conveyed by the text's content. Encourage them to ask, "How can I make this text come to life, evoking an emotion in my audience?"

6. Model a text slam for students.

7. Invite students to choose a favorite text.

8. Provide time for students to prepare their own read-aloud performances during silent reading and the individual practice portion of readers' workshop.

9. Prepare a special time each day and an area of the room for readings to be performed.

10. Offer a schedule for students to sign up for a text slam performance.

Peering into the Classroom

Lois's fifth graders saunter back into the room returning from afternoon recess. They sit down in anticipation of her reading aloud to them and their own independent silent reading. Standing next to a single text propped on the table at the front of the classroom, Lois begins.

"Today we are going to do something different during read-aloud and silent reading. We are going to begin an activity called Text Slam. A text slam is an opportunity for us to celebrate reading." Pausing to build student anticipation, she picks up the text from the table beside her. She continues, "I want you each to choose a text that gets you excited about reading. You will increase your reading comprehension and reading fluency as you prepare to share your text with others. You will also improve your listening comprehension as you experience your classmates' performances, and develop your desire to read for pleasure!"

"How is this different from our regular afternoon reading time?" Erin inquires.

"Good question, Erin," Lois states. "Usually during silent reading, you read to yourselves and write in your response log. In a text slam you *perform* a part of one of your favorite texts."

"What do you mean by *perform*?" Lisa asks. "Do we act it out, kind of like a play?"

"Not exactly," answers Lois. "You will perform this read-aloud in much the same way that you would in Readers Theater. In a text slam you first read the text to yourselves and use your understanding of it to determine how to read it aloud so that others will become interested in it."

"Do we get to read *anything* we want to the class?" Erin asks.

"Yes, Erin," says Lois. "But, you may want to choose a text that allows you to convey a particular emotion or evoke a strong reaction from the audience." Lois holds up her book and continues. "I chose this text because it includes one of my favorite poems, *The Jabberwocky*. I love it because it is mysterious and the poem's content will allow me to show my comprehension by varying my pace and reading it with expression. I also chose this text because I think you will enjoy it. Let me show you what I mean."

Lois opens the book and says, "When I chose this text, I asked myself how I might bring the Jabberwocky to life as I read it aloud." She begins her performance. Lois reads slowly, enunciating each word clearly. While reading, she meanders throughout the islands of desks, hunched and lunging from side to side congruent with the content. Students gaze and listen appreciatively as the performance continues.

After the reading, Lois invites her students to locate a favorite text to prepare for their own text slams. Lois circulates around the room to offer support to striving readers as needed. Students continue practicing their read-alouds for the remainder of individual reading time. As the period concludes, Lois says, "We will devote a special time each day for you to perform your text slams beginning tomorrow afternoon. When you are ready, you may volunteer to perform your text by signing your name on the sign-up sheet. Remember that your goal is to bring your text to life so that others will be able to enjoy and comprehend what you are reading."

Text Suggestions

- *The Big Fat Cow That Goes Kapow* by Andy Griffiths
- *Don't Say That Word!* by Alan Katz
- *Incredible Inventions* by Lee Bennett Hopkins
- *Me and My Animal Friends* by Ralph Covert
- *Rhyming Dust Bunnies* by Jan Thomas
- *Robot Zot* by Jon Scieszka
- *The Underwear Salesman* by J. Patrick Lewis

Extension Ideas

★ One way to extend the fun of text slam is to play "Name That Text!" Challenge students during readers' workshop to select a portion of text from a familiar book. Ask students to choose a few paragraphs that aren't completely obscure, but that don't give the secret of the text away immediately. Have them practice the text until they are comfortable reading it aloud, and then play Name That Text! Ask the listening students to wait until the reader is finished before they guess what book the text comes from. Allow the reader to give hints if needed.

★ Not only do great texts inspire, they also unite. Consider a "Book Idol" contest, modeled after the TV show *American Idol*. Students may each nominate one of their favorite books to be a contestant on Book Idol. A nomination would include a write-up of why it should "make it to Hollywood" (or to the next round) and a practiced oral read of a portion of the text. Stress to students that this isn't a popularity contest of the person nominating the book, but a test of the appeal of the book to a wide variety of people. Students can "text their vote" to the teacher (holding up a sign or filling out a form), narrowing the field to ten books, then to five, and so on. As a student's book makes it through each round, she or he will need to read a different portion of the text or highlight a different part of why it should be chosen, until one classroom favorite is crowned the winner of the competition.

CHAPTER 5

Writing Strategies

On the way to school, the light turns red and I (Roland) look over to see my son writing in his poetry journal. Later that evening, in our established "books on bed" routine, I read a poem to him. He declared, "Hey, that poem sounds a lot like some of the poems I wrote in my poetry book!" Just as Jeannette Veatch said years ago, "Reading and writing are two sides of the same coin" (1979). Reading and writing have a reciprocal relationship and provide insights to both processes for striving readers. With this natural relationship between reading and writing in mind, we put forward these five reasons for using authentic writing activities to support the development of striving readers.

★ *Writing and reading are naturally connected.* For instance, reading with a pencil in hand and writing comments to the author or ourselves is a natural occurrence for many readers. This interaction between the reader and the writer forges the reading-writing connection, making both necessary for understanding.

★ *Teaching writing and reading together make both more accessible.* Learning how to write and studying the writing craft informs the process for learning to read. Reading like a writer allows a striving reader to understand reading from the inside out. Just as writers use prewriting, writing, and post-writing strategies for creating meaning, readers use similar strategies before, during, and after reading to understand the text.

Reading Skills	Focused Writers' Workshop	Read-Aloud Free Response	Two-Column Notes	Language Experience Approach (LEA)	Directed Writing-Thinking Activity (DW-TA)
reading interest	●	●	●	●	●
seeing text as accessible			●	●	●
fluency		●		●	
predicting		●	●		●
summarizing			●	●	●
connecting	●	●	●	●	
questioning	●		●		●
synthesizing		●	●	●	
inferring		●	●		
visualizing		●			●
monitoring comprehension	●	●	●		
determining importance	●	●	●	●	●
listening comprehension		●	●	●	●
gathering facts		●	●	●	●
social vocabulary					
academic vocabulary	●		●	●	
sequence of events	●	●	●	●	●

Figure 5.1. Writing teaching strategies and the reading skills they nurture

★ *Writing enables children to interact with text in a variety of ways to enhance understanding.* Depending on the genre or structure of a text, striving readers may draw from a number of writing activities to respond to a text (e.g., semantic webs, list-group-label, two-column notes, etc.). Explicitly taught written response activities enhance striving readers' comprehension monitoring.

★ *Writing helps readers make sense of reading.* Writing, the active effort to compose, supports reading, the active effort to understand. A writer uses prewriting to create background knowledge, whereas a reader uses the parallel act of prereading to activate background knowledge. In understanding the process for constructing a message by creating connections between information, a reader can then monitor understanding while reading by considering how information is linked. After writing, a writer employs reading strategies to determine whether he or she succeeded in stating the intended message.

★ *Children learn best when using both writing and reading to explore topics of interest.* Tapping into children's natural desire to write involves writing about what they know. We write to understand ourselves. The same goes for reading. Readers desire personal and interpersonal connections to what they are reading. Writing and reading about topics of interest nurtures both in tandem.

Mindful of these five reasons, we posit five ways to use writing to enhance reading ability. Figure 5.1 shows these teaching strategies and the skills they elicit.

FOCUSED WRITERS' WORKSHOP

Description: One of the ways that students learn to write is by writing about themselves and their experiences. As students use their own writing to learn the craft and mechanics of writing, learning about writing becomes natural and authentic. Focused Writers' Workshop provides the structure for the teacher to scaffold the writing process and honor the writing desire of striving readers. It encourages students to take ownership of their writing.

The four-part workshop begins with a brief, teacher-directed lesson presented to the whole class. Personal writing time follows, during which students write with a common focus (e.g., genre, topic, theme, shared experience, or using a particular literary element).

The third part, which is naturally intermingled with personal silent writing time, includes time for striving readers to revise their writing. It is an opportunity for the writer to review and reread to make sense of the writing. During silent writing and revision, the teacher conferences with individuals or small groups to assess writing progress and provide further instruction as necessary. The workshop concludes with student sharing in pairs or small groups followed by whole-class sharing and wrap-up.

Teaching Suggestions

1. Plan the teacher-directed mini-lesson, conferencing schedule, and the whole-group wrap-up activity according to students' strengths, needs, and interests as identified by previous writing experiences.

2. Select a focus for the writing lesson. Keep in mind the varying levels of student ability and interest. Display the focus on a piece of chart paper for all to see.

3. Invite students to use an existing piece of writing or begin a new project depending on the nature of the mini-lesson. For instance, focus on rereading an existing project to identify and replace overused or general verbs.

4. State the purpose of the teacher-directed mini-lesson. You might state something such as, "This lesson is intended to help you identify and, if necessary, replace verbs in your stories. As you reread a story that you have been crafting, explore opportunities for replacing your verbs with more descriptive, vivid verbs."

5. Teach the mini-lesson. Read aloud a portion of your own writing or an authentic text to model general possibilities or specific examples. For example, use a teacher-created narrative to model using vivid verbs.

6. Encourage students to ask questions for clarification.

7. Invite students to begin writing. Instruct them to reread their writing to attend to the focus of the mini-lesson and to make any necessary changes. Model the process with some of your own writing. Use conferences with individuals and small groups to assess student understanding.

Lesson Focus

The teacher, the whole class, or a small group of students may determine the lesson focus. It may be based on students' strengths, needs, interests, or a combination of the three.

Teacher as Writer

Teacher writing and sharing allows students to relate to the teacher as a writer and vicariously experience the steps of the writing process.

8. Allow students to work in pairs or small groups for a specified amount of time after the individual writing period has ended. Encourage students to extend their understanding by discussing their ideas and processes.

9. Invite students to come together for whole-group sharing and the lesson wrap-up.

Peering into the Classroom

Debbie's fourth graders have been learning how to make their writing more descriptive. Debbie decides to enhance student understanding of descriptive writing by teaching a mini-lesson on word choice, more specifically, on using vivid verbs. The scaffolded support and opportunities to interact with peers makes Focused Writers' Workshop the perfect activity for nurturing a community of writers and supporting striving readers.

As students ready themselves for writers' workshop, Debbie comments, "Writers' workshop is going to be a little different today; it's going to be a little more focused. For this Focused Writers' Workshop, I am going to show you a specific writing and revision technique that you can use as writers. After conferencing with each of you over the last week, I have realized that some focused attention on word choice could make your stories more descriptive. In particular, today we are going to work on using vivid verbs to make your writing more exciting."

"So, today you will need to choose a text that you have already begun. The purpose of this lesson is to get you to think about alternative verbs that will make your writing more descriptive. Focusing on the same writing goal will allow all of you to share and discuss your stories throughout the process. When you share, you will be able to focus on one another's use of vivid verbs and learn from one another," explains Debbie.

She begins the mini-lesson by reading some of her own writing aloud in the author's chair. Before beginning the reading she says, "Please listen to my story and identify any verbs that are overused or those that are general. Jot each one down on a separate sticky note. After I finish reading my story two times, you will get to post your sticky notes up on the board under the title of my story, 'Super Chicken Learns to Fly'."

Debbie reads her short story aloud, demonstrating fluent reading. She reads rapidly as action builds and with oral interpretation to showcase character voices and personalities. Debbie pauses after the first reading and is elated to see many students jotting down verbs. Following the second reading, Debbie invites students to post

Conferencing Schedule

Meeting with each student once a week ensures that time is being allocated to individual practice and allows us to monitor student progress and support students one on one.

their verbs on the whiteboard at the front of the classroom. She wanders over and chooses one of the many verbs identified.

"Kalee has written 'learns, from the title' on this sticky. What do you suppose would be a vivid alternative to *learns*? Please turn and discuss your ideas with a neighbor," Debbie requests as she begins to circulate the room, listening in on student conversations. After a minute, she asks, "What did you come up with?"

"I think that *learns* could be replaced with *soars* because it makes sense with the story and it is alliterative," offers Andrea.

"Wow! *Soars* is a vivid verb. It certainly does make sense based on what we know about Super Chicken from the story," Debbie remarks. "This is exactly what you will do as you reread your own stories. You will identify the verbs that you used. You may write them on sticky notes or simply create a list. After you finish reading, take time to consider vivid alternatives for your verbs that will make your story more descriptive. Make the appropriate changes in your stories. Then, after you spend time working to identify and change verbs in your own writing, I will signal you to work with a partner to discuss possible changes in each other's stories."

Debbie invites students to begin reading their writing. She circulates through the room to check on individuals who may need clarification, modeling, or further support. After 20 minutes of individual practice, she signals writers to begin working with a partner. Debbie moves from pair to pair assessing student collaboration and understanding by listening in on their conversations. After five minutes, she calls the students together. Once volunteers have shared several examples of vivid verbs, she closes the lesson by saying, "Remember, many writers use vivid verbs to help readers visualize and understand the intended message. Now that you are more aware of using writing to enhance readers' understanding, today you can read like a writer to see how another author uses vivid verbs to enhance *your* understanding."

Text Suggestions

- *Bag in the Wind* by Ted Kooser
- *Big Chickens Go to Town* by Leslie Helakoski
- *The Inside Tree* by Linda Smith
- *Nothing Scares Us* by Frieda Wishinsky
- *A Verb for Herb* by Maria Fleming
- *Which Puppy?* by Kate Feiffer
- *Young Zeus* by G. Brian Karas

Extension Ideas

★ Encourage students to look through their writing to find examples of a specific area of growth that they can write on sentence strips to hang on the wall or on a bulletin board. For the verb example, they could find three verbs that they changed in their writing. In partners, they could read their three changes and decide which one was the most powerful. Once they have decided, they could use the following template to fill out their sentence strip. "At first I said _____, (write old word here in blue) but now I say _____." (new word here in red). Not only are students seeing individual growth in word choice, but they are seeing other strong student examples modeled for them.

★ Asking students to read like writers scaffolds their knowledge of the components of good writing. Providing access to trade books that serve as mentor texts for the focus of the workshop gives students concrete examples of what they are striving for in their writing. Give each group of four students a book that showcases strong examples of the focus. Continuing with the verb example, you could pass out *A Verb for Herb, Nothing Scares Us, The Inside Tree,* and *Bag in the Wind.* Have each group choose a book to share. Then ask one person in the group to write down all the verbs from the page of the text they've chosen. Out of that list, instruct them that they need to choose the verb they all agree is the strongest, and that is their "winner verb." Groups can share their winners with the class by reading them in the context of the sentences. Once they've shared, ask them to think about trying to use "winner verbs" in their writing that day.

READ-ALOUD FREE RESPONSE

Description: Reading aloud authentic texts is one way to showcase models of writing. Not only does reading aloud expose students to and nurture interest in a variety of texts, but a purposefully chosen text can be useful for revealing explicit models of writing, writing techniques, genres, or text structures. Furthermore, having students write or draw in response to a read-aloud is one way to draw their attention to specific text structures.

Read-Aloud Free Response is one way for striving readers to use teacher-modeled reading experiences to make sense of the writing process. The teacher reads aloud a purposefully chosen text as a vehicle for helping students with their writing. Striving readers are given a purpose for listening (e.g., listen for text organization, interesting ideas or facts, character descriptions, or specific grammar use). The teacher pauses periodically to allow striving readers to write or draw about specific examples identified in the text.

Teaching Suggestions

1. Identify a particular student writing need from writing conferences and other performance-based writing assessments. With the writing need in mind, identify a text to read aloud to showcase appropriate uses of the writing element in need.

> ### Offering Writing Support
>
> *Giving one-on-one instruction and participating in the writing process yourself offer two ways to support writers during individual practice.*

2. Share the purpose of Read-Aloud Free Response with students. You might say, "The purpose of this activity is to allow you to strategically listen to the text that I read aloud to identify any examples of personification. I will stop reading at strategic points in the text to allow you to reflect on examples of personification by writing or drawing."

3. Model the procedure. Begin by reading a portion of the text aloud, stopping after the first example of personification. Display the text large enough for all to see. Write the example (e.g., *the wind carried the baseball out of the stadium*), or sketch a picture of the wind carrying the baseball over the outfield fence. Continue modeling as necessary until students express the desire to perform the Read-Aloud Free Response on their own.

4. Continue reading the text, stopping frequently to allow students to practice responding.

5. Circulate among the students to assess student understanding and to offer support to individuals as necessary.

6. Invite students to share their responses with a neighbor or the whole class.

7. Continue the process until students show that they can independently identify models of the element being studied.

8. Invite students to begin reading their own texts to identify examples of the writing element.

9. Extend the activity by encouraging students to create their own examples of the writing element in their own writing.

Peering into the Classroom

Terri's fifth graders have been using literary elements (e.g., simile, metaphor, onomatopoeia) in their stories to make them more animated. She has been conferencing with them over the last few days during writers' workshop to assess their use of expressive writing and to explore their thinking as writers. Terri has found that many striving readers need support using literary elements to make their writing more descriptive. She decides to look at the types of texts they are reading to identify student interest in these elements. Terri's inquiry helps her to see that her striving readers enjoy reading texts that incorporate personification. She decides to use Read-Aloud Free Response to offer scaffolded practice of personification. Having found an appropriate text, Terri explains, "The purpose of this lesson is to allow you to strategically listen to the text that I read aloud for examples of personification. I will stop reading at times to allow you to write or draw them. I'll show you how."

Terri continues by reading the text aloud until she comes to the first example of personification. On an overhead transparency, Terri writes the example, "the moon's gaze followed me across the meadow." She thinks aloud, "I think I will sketch that because I have a vivid image in my mind." Terri sketches the image. She then continues reading until she comes to another example of personification. She writes, "The wind tugged at my cloak" and says, "I think I will describe what that means to me in writing." Terri writes an explanation of the strength of the wind and the effect it had on the character. "Now it is your turn to do as I just did as you listen for examples of personification."

Terri continues reading the text, stopping at examples of personification to allow for student response. As students respond, she circulates among them and offers support as necessary. Occasionally, she models the process again by creating her own response on the board. Every so often, Terri invites her students to turn-talk-and-listen to share their thinking and responses with a neighbor or the whole group.

Terri and her fifth graders continue until she feels that all have demonstrated their ability to identify personification. Closing the text, she says, "Now I would like you to create your own examples of personification."

Students immediately begin writing. Terri navigates her way around the classroom to assess and support individual students as needed. With some, she leans over to take a peek at their progress. With others, she pulls up a chair to conference and offer support.

After all students have had adequate time to apply their learning by writing, Terri invites them to share their examples with a peer while she circulates to listen in on students' conversations to assess their understanding and writing progress. After a few minutes, she brings them together as a whole group to share a few examples and wrap up.

"Would anyone like to share?" Terri inquires.

"The colorful birthday cake called to me from the top of the fridge," chimes Jasmine.

"What does that mean?" Terri asks. "Turn and talk to your table group about Jasmine's example of personification." After a short period of time, Terri asks, "So, what do you think?"

"It means that Jasmine really wanted the cake," explains Jessie.

"So remember, paying attention to how authors craft their writing will help you to make sense of their writing. You can learn to use the same skills when you write. When you are reading today, be on the lookout for examples of personification and consider how the author uses them to make the text more animated and more descriptive. Jot those ideas down in your reading journals so that you can refer to them when you are doing your own writing."

Text Suggestions

- *Abe Lincoln: The Boy Who Loved Books* by Kay Winters
- *The Big Orange Splot* by Daniel Manus Pinkwater
- *Butterflies for Kiri* by Cathryn Falwell
- *Fletcher and the Springtime Blossoms* by Julia Rawlinson
- *It's Picture Day Today!* by Megan McDonald
- *Raspberries!* by Jay O'Callahan
- *Starring Lorenzo and Einstein Too* by Mark Karlins

Extension Ideas

★ Taking the examples of personification students heard during the read-aloud a step further, ask if they can extend them. For example, when the phrase "the moon's gaze followed me across the meadow" is read aloud, stop and ask students to think of another personification that could be given to the moon within the context of the story, modeling a sentence like "the moon's gaze was pointed on me like a spotlight."

★ Help students understand that authors use personification directly and indirectly. For example, texts such as *The Little House* or *Mike Mulligan and His Steam Shovel* by Virginia Lee Burton provide explicit examples. They feature an inanimate object, a house, and a steam shovel, given obvious human qualities throughout the book. Contrast these examples with others, such as *Fletcher and the Springtime Blossoms* by Julia Rawlinson or *Abe Lincoln* by Kay Winters, where personification is used in a less obvious manner. After reading books aloud that illustrate how much or little personification is used, ask students whether it was a main part of the story or a technique the author used to make a sentence or two more interesting. Help students to conclude that they can also choose how much or how little they would like to include such techniques in their stories.

TWO-COLUMN NOTES

Description: Using Two-Column Notes provides one way for striving readers to monitor their comprehension by writing during and after reading. It is a strategy for connecting, questioning, predicting, inferring, synthesizing, and determining the importance of what is read. When taught explicitly, Two-Column Notes allows a structure for interacting with any text (narrative, informational, poetry, etc.). The information listed in the left-hand column is directly associated with the information across from it in the right-hand column. For example, the left-hand column may be used for questions about the text and the right side used to record answers found while reading. Or, the left may be used for key words and the right used to record definitions stated in the text. Teaching the strategy, explaining how it will help students, thinking aloud while modeling it, and providing guided practice over time will help striving readers use it to gain the most from their reading.

Teaching Suggestions

1. Choose an interesting text that will allow you to model the use of two-column notes.
2. Explain the purpose of the activity—for readers to keep track of their thinking during and after reading.
3. Invite students to fold or draw a line down the middle of a piece of paper lengthwise. Show them a model of two-column notes that you have prepared on chart paper.
4. Explain the process for using the strategy. The left-hand column may include a list of key vocabulary words found in the text. The right-hand column would then include information found in the text to define each word.
5. Provide a copy of the text to each student.
6. Ask the students to brainstorm key vocabulary associated with the topic by using their background knowledge. Record their ideas on the left side of your

Vocabulary	Definitions From the Text
Reptile	
Amphibian	
Cold-blooded	

Figure 5.2. "Two-Column Notes: Reptiles"

"Two-Column Notes" chart. Add any terms that you think might add to their understanding of the text.

7. Read a section of the text aloud. Stop when you come to key information that defines a word on your "Two-Column Notes." Think aloud while writing the information in the right-hand column, directly across from the word being defined.

8. Invite students to write the information on their individual two-column note charts.

9. Continue reading, using think-alouds when stopping to record defining information, until students are prepared to take over.

10. Encourage students to work individually or with a partner to read the text and record information. If time allows, invite them to add other vocabulary terms of interest and their definitions found in the text. Circulate the room, attending to striving readers to assess understanding and offer support as necessary.

11. Call students together, inviting them to share and discuss their discoveries.

Peering into the Classroom

Roger knows that teaching his striving third-grade readers to monitor their comprehension while reading is one of the keys to their reading success. He has decided to teach them how to use two-column notes to track their thinking. For an example, he is using an informational text about reptiles, and he has prepared a visual of Two-Column Notes on chart paper (see Figure 5.2).

As writers' workshop begins, Roger explains the purpose of the day's mini-lesson, saying, "Today I am going to teach you how to use a writing strategy called Two-Column Notes to help you understand what you are reading. First, I need you to fold or draw a line down the middle of a piece of paper lengthwise like this," Roger says, pointing to his two-column notes visual. He walks around the room to assist individual students as they prepare their charts.

When students are ready, he says, "I am going to read aloud from *Everything Reptile: What Kids Really Want to Know About Reptiles* by Cherie Winner. While I read, I am going to show you how I use two-column notes to track my thinking and understand key vocabulary. On the left side of the paper I will write key vocabulary words associated with reptiles, either drawn from background knowledge or from the text." Roger writes "Vocabulary" on the top of the left-hand column and motions for students to do the same. "Please follow along by writing the same information in the same places on your two-column notes."

"I need your help to identify some key vocabulary," explains Roger, as he passes out photocopies of the text to each student. "What are some terms that we might need to know to make sense of this text as we read?"

"We need to know what a reptile is," offers Sergio, looking at the title of the text.

"Yes, that would be helpful," Roger says, writing the word *reptile* in the left-hand column.

Other students volunteer. "I don't know the difference between a reptile and an amphibian," shares Alejandra as she leafs through the pages of the text. "I would like to know what an amphibian is. The text has information about amphibians right here," she says, pointing to the text.

"We will write *amphibian* right here, part way down the left column under *reptile*, says Roger. "I want to know what cold-blooded means. I have heard that term associated with reptiles. I am going to write the word *cold-blooded* toward the bottom of the left-hand column." Roger takes a quick walk around the classroom to peek at student notes and offer clarification as necessary.

"We will use the right side to write information we find in the text that helps us to define each vocabulary term and title it "Definitions From the Text." I will record this information as I come to it during my read-aloud. Please follow along. You may read silently or just listen for helpful information as I read aloud."

Roger reads aloud until he comes to information defining the word *reptile*. He stops reading and shares his thinking using think-aloud. "The text says that reptiles are covered with dry scales that may be smooth or bumpy, and reptiles are not slimy. This helps me to understand what a *reptile* is so I am going to write *covered with smooth or bumpy scales* and *not slimy* in the right column directly across from the vocabulary word *reptile*." The third graders mimic the note taking. Roger continues reading until he reveals information that defines the characteristics of an amphibian. Thinking aloud, he records that information in the right column across from the vocabulary word *amphibian*. Roger circulates around the room to assess student progress and understanding by looking at their notes.

"It looks like you know how to use this strategy to interact with the text and keep track of your thinking. You may work individually or with a partner to read for a definition of *cold-blooded*. After you have found that definition and have recorded it, see if you can determine other important vocabulary that you need defined to enhance your understanding of what you are reading. Please follow the same process for recording information."

After several minutes, Roger calls students together. He invites individuals to share the definitions they found of *cold-blooded* and any other vocabulary they have discovered. A brief whole-class discussion ensues. To close, Roger says, "Using Two-Column Notes allows you to understand important vocabulary so you can comprehend what you are reading. Give it a try today while you are reading silently."

Text Suggestions

- *The Bug Book* by Maria Fleming
- *Everything Reptile: What Kids Really Want to Know About Reptiles* by Cherie Winner
- *Fancy Nancy: Poet Extraordinaire!* by Jane O'Connor
- *Flanimals* by Ricky Gervais
- *A Kick in the Head* by Paul B. Janeczko
- *The Plot Chickens* by Mary Jane and Herb Auch
- *This Is Your Life Cycle* by Heather Lynn Miller

Extension Ideas

★ If the *Everything Reptile* (Winner) book is generating sustained interest, use it for more exposure to the Two-Column Note idea. It could be extended to include three columns and used to work on a different strategy, such as prediction. Pass out a premade table (or have students make their own) that has three columns.

The first column would be labeled "Question." The second column would be labeled "Prediction" and the third column would be labeled "Answer," as modeled below.

Question	Prediction	Answer

Using the book's table of contents, read aloud some questions such as "Can lizards walk on water?" Have students write down selected questions, and then write their prediction in the next column. They will then listen in the text for the answer, which they will record on their sheet.

★ Two-column notes naturally lend themselves to evaluation in which readers are encouraged to think like writers to determine if the author's style of writing works for them. This can be open-ended or more focused, depending on the objective. Consider using a humorous book like *This Is Your Life Cycle* by Heather Lynn Miller or *The Plot Chickens* by Mary Jane and Herb Auch to evaluate the effectiveness of the author's use of humor using the Two-Column Note method. In the first column, students write down a quote or a description of a humorous attempt by the author. In the second column, students write their reaction, possibly including why it was effective (or not!) for them as a reader (see example below).

Quote (with page number)	My Reaction
Pg. 5 The bugs in the audience are doing a cheer, saying "Give me a G! Give me an O! GO! GO! GO, Dahlia!"	Bugs doing a cheer make me laugh. Some have several arms raised, which is funny because we only have two arms.

LANGUAGE EXPERIENCE APPROACH (LEA)

Description: The Language Experience Approach (LEA) is an integrated literacy approach that purposefully combines listening, speaking, reading, and writing to facilitate reading growth. Grounded in the work of Roach Van Allen in 1976, the approach still has merit today. In fact, it is often deemed as a cornerstone of emergent literacy instruction. LEA is based on these learner perspectives:

- My thinking about my experiences is important.
- I can talk about my thinking.
- What I talk about may be written by myself or others.
- I can read my language that has been written.

LEA provides a personal and motivating way to teach literacy by focusing on individual experiences and the personal language used to describe those experiences.

LEA provides one highly engaging way for striving readers to develop reading skills. Using an individual's own language to scaffold the process for developing written accounts of personal experience ultimately allows him or her to read those accounts. The process begins with a highly engaging personal learning experience (e.g., field trip or interactive learning activity). A conversation using the language appropriate to the learning experience follows. Students then dictate their account of the language experience as their words are recorded for all to see. While writing the story, the teacher thinks aloud while addressing key reading skills.

> ### Teachable Moments
>
> *The teacher can take the opportunity to address skills such as beginning and ending letter sounds, using punctuation, and identifying high-frequency words, all the while attending to and using the learners' language.*

The teacher then reads through the story several times while pointing to each word as it is read. Students then read the story aloud several times as the teacher points to the words. Lastly, the teacher makes the text available to all students to practice reading on their own.

Teaching Suggestions

1. Link the LEA lesson to a highly engaging personal learning experience. Examples include: a field trip to the pet store, an interactive demonstration by a guest presenter, a hands-on science experiment, an art activity, and so on.

2. Initiate a student-led conversation about the experience. Incorporate key vocabulary into the conversation if students do not. For example, after touring a candy factory, you might say, "What were the materials and the steps of the process for making candy canes?"

3. Inform students that the purpose of the LEA is to allow them to create a story of their experience using their own words. Tell them that you will write their story down as they create it and then you will read it aloud several times so that they can read it by themselves.

4. Encourage striving readers to dictate the story as you record it large enough for all to see. Help them dictate the story in complete sentences. Using student language with as little correction as possible in order to make it *their* story is critical. It is also important to keep the story as brief as possible.

5. Present or reinforce beginning reading skills as opportunities arise. For instance, identify high-frequency words or academic language that is used by students as they dictate their story.

6. Read the story aloud to students several times by placing your hand or a pointer under each word as it is read.

7. Invite students to read the story aloud several times with you. Be sure to continue pointing to each word or phrase as it is read aloud.

8. Encourage individuals or groups of students to reread their story in the days to follow.

9. Extend the activity by duplicating the text, or getting students to rewrite the text, into individual books for students to read on their own or take home to read to family members.

Text Length

The length of the text created by the students is dependent upon how it will be used. Expecting students to read their story independently after it is has been written, modeled, and practiced with teacher support require it to be limited to two to four sentences for kindergartners and progressively longer for more experienced readers. The size of the story will also vary based on the size of the group dictating the story.

Peering into the Classroom

Todd believes that his striving kindergarten readers can learn how to read by using their language skills in listening and speaking. Knowing the importance of using personal experiences for developing the language skills of emerging readers, Todd decides to capitalize on the recent science observation activity involving the eating habits of the class pet, a box turtle named Lightning.

As the kindergartners return from recess and take their seats, Todd says, "Turn-talk-and-listen to a neighbor as you discuss your experience observing the eating habits of our classroom pet, Lightning." Todd circulates around the room as students engage in conversations about their experiences. He listens in to get a feel for their level of interest and ability to verbally share their experiences with one another.

After approximately five minutes, Todd brings the class together by inviting them to join him on the rug in front of the writing easel. He exclaims, "It sounds like you were very interested in our observations of the turtle! Not only that, you appear to have learned a lot! You are able to talk about your experience. Today we are going to use your words to write about this experience. The purpose is for you to use your own ideas and words to create a class experience story. Remember that you will need to take turns telling me what to write so I can write out all of your great ideas," Todd says, as he points to the blank chart paper propped beside him. "After I write the story that you create, I will read it aloud to you several times while you watch me point to each word. Then you will get to read it aloud with me. We will do all of this so that you will be able to read the story on your own later."

"How would you like to begin this story?" Todd asks.

"What does the box turtle like to eat?" says MaryJo.

Todd writes the sentence on the chart large enough for all to see and says, "We will end that sentence with a question mark since that is a question."

"Our class wanted to find out what Lightning's favorite foods are by feeding him different things," Tanner includes. Todd records the end of Tanner's sentence and continues to write student thinking, as depicted below.

What does the box turtle like to eat?

We tried feeding him different things.

He likes to eat bananas and strawberries.

It is cool to watch him eat.

After completing the chart, Todd says, "Now I am going to read through your ideas, pointing to each word. I would like you to watch and listen carefully as I read." Todd reads through the list of sentences a few times as students focus on how each word sounds and what it looks like in writing. After performing the second read-aloud, Todd states, "Now I would like you to read with me as I point to each word. The class reads chorally, attending to each word. After several successful readings, Todd states, "Now you should know the text well enough to try reading it on your own. Your story will be up here for you to use during independent reading time."

Text Suggestions

- *Alexander and the Terrible, Horrible, No Good, Very Bad Day* by Judith Viorst
- *Field Trip Day* by Lynn Plourde
- *I'm Small and Other Verses* by Lilian Moore
- *Insect Detective* by Steve Voake
- *Stampede!* by Laura Purdie Salas
- *Thunder-Boomer!* by Shutta Crum
- *Winter: An Alphabet Acrostic* by Steven Schnur

Extension Ideas

★ One way to bring LEA into the classroom regularly is to weave it into the daily routine. A morning message or daily news chart can be co-constructed to tie the classroom community together. To help ensure success for early readers, repeat the same introductory sentences, such as "Today is Monday. We go to art," and then leave room for a third sentence that students will construct. Either the class can negotiate what will go next, such as "It is snowing today!" or the designated news reporter for the day can choose the next sentence, such as "Matt lost a tooth last night!" If the class decides, copies can be made and each member could take the daily news sheet home that night. If the news reporter comes up with the language, he or she would take it home.

★ Using books as models to be rewritten can take on many different forms. Reading aloud the book *Alexander and the Terrible, Horrible, No Good, Very Bad Day* by Judith Viorst lends itself to a discussion of bad days and to recording students' terrible, horrible, no good, very bad days. Write their words in a sentence or two on the bottom of a blank piece of paper and ask them to illustrate it, Collect their pages and assemble them into a class book.

★ Consider using a book such as *Insect Detective* by Steve Voake to introduce the idea that insects are hiding everywhere. Take the class outside to hunt for insects. Once they return to the room, provide time for each to dictate sentences that could be written on shapes that resemble the insects they discovered. An example would be "I am an insect detective. I found a busy ant," written on an ant made out of construction paper. Display the writing for all to read.

DIRECTED WRITING-THINKING ACTIVITY (DW-TA)

Description: The Directed Reading-Thinking Activity (DR-TA) involves setting purposes before, during, and after reading to guide student thinking and promote reading comprehension. Originally created by Stauffer (1968), the DR-TA is a mainstay of literacy programs. We believe that the basic tenets of the model can be used for writing as a way to support striving readers.

The Directed Writing-Thinking Activity (DW-TA) helps students set purposes for their writing. It is particularly well suited to both narrative and informational writing. It encourages the writer to communicate effectively with his or her audience by acting as a reader. Through rereading, students plan their writing, attending to the predictive qualities of their text.

In a DW-TA, the author must consider the reader's expectations when forming a purpose for writing the text. For instance, after creating the title, pictures, and subtitles that go along with the intended text, the writer uses them to predict what the text will be about from the reader's perspective. At this point, the writer may record ideas about the text in a chart or a semantic map, as a reader would do. The writer then writes the text, verifying given reading predictions. The writer may include information in his or her writing that allows the reader to verify predictions, summarize what has been read, and make further predictions about what might happen next in the text. In essence, striving readers use reading skills to guide their writing strategies.

Teaching Suggestions

1. Inform students of the purpose for the DW-TA— to think like readers as they create a text as writers.

2. Describe the DW-TA to students. It is a process for writing that allows writers to

use reading skills and strategies to set purposes for their writing. For example, readers naturally make predictions while reading a text to monitor understanding and to think ahead and decide what might happen next in the text. By attending to this reading strategy, writers can guide their readers by creating a text that allows them to predict and verify or disprove predictions throughout the reading.

3. Tell students that you will be assisting them as they perform both processes for reading and writing as they create an informational text.

4. Encourage students to determine a topic of interest. Invite students to prewrite by creating a title, illustrations, and subheadings for each section of their informational texts.

5. Instruct students to act as a reader would by prereading. It may be appropriate to have them think like their classmates as they read. Have them view the title, illustrations, and subheadings and make predictions based on their observations. They may use a table, semantic web, or a "What do you . . ." chart like the one below to record their ideas as a reader would.

What do you . . .		
know?	**want to know?**	**think you will learn?**

6. Ask students to attend to the information in the chart as they think like a writer. Understanding what their peers know about a particular topic will allow them to write about what they may want to know and think they will learn. This will help writers create their texts with the purpose of providing new information for their readers.

7. Invite students to write with the purpose of providing new and interesting information for their intended audience. Conference one-on-one with students to support their written ideas as necessary.

8. Encourage students to continuously reread to attend to the needs of their readers and rewrite accordingly. Showcase the process for reading and making predictions as a reader would do while experiencing their texts. Model the process if necessary with individual striving readers, small groups, or the whole class.

9. Invite students to exchange their drafts with a partner to offer and collect feedback on their writing. Have readers follow the process for the Directed Reading-Thinking Activity by having them fill out their own "What do you . . ." chart during prereading. You may have students follow an alternative procedure during review by having them pose questions for one another to guide further revisions by using the prompt guide below.

Prompts Used for Peer Review

I already knew . . .

I didn't know . . .

I wanted to know . . .

I learned . . .

I thought I would learn . . .

---

10. Provide time for students to continue rewriting, rereading, and peer-reviewing to complete their drafts. Encourage students to share their drafts with the whole group in the author's chair or in small groups around the room.

Peering into the Classroom

Jenny believes that one of the best ways to support reading and writing development of her fourth graders is to integrate the two throughout the curriculum. For this reason she uses the DW-TA on a regular basis during writers' workshop.

Today, Jenny begins by stating, "We have been using the DR-TA to guide us as readers. Today we are going to use the prereading, reading, and post-reading to help us grow as writers. We will use the Directed Writing-Thinking Activity to create an informational text. The purpose is to think like a reader as you create a text as a writer."

Jenny asks, "What is the purpose for using the DR-TA?"

"We use it to make predictions before and during reading," explains Josh.

"Exactly. By making predictions you are able to monitor your understanding of the text and make predictions of what you think might be discussed later on in the text," Jenny affirms. "By attending to this *reading* strategy when writing, you can guide your readers by creating a text that allows them to predict and verify or disprove predictions before, during, and after they read. Today you will begin creating an informational text using both processes. I will be coming around to conference with you to help you as you do so."

Jenny encourages students to identify a topic they want to write about. She invites them to perform a prewrite by creating a title, several rough illustrations, and subheadings for the texts they plan to write. She then circulates the room attending to individuals and table groups as necessary to monitor their understanding and provide guidance.

After ten minutes Jenny addresses the whole class. "Now that you have a plan for your writing, I want you to act like a reader and pre-read by viewing your own title, illustrations, and subheadings and make predictions based on your observations. You may decide to use a table, semantic web, or a 'What do you . . .' chart to record your ideas."

"You want us to act like a reader and use the information we created to make predictions?" Kirsten inquires.

"Yes. May I see your prewrite? Kirsten, I see that you have created a title, a few illustrations, and several subheadings about petunias. This is a great idea because we have recently talked about petunias and other flowers when you planted a daisy for your mothers to give them for Mother's Day. You will now act as a reader would to view those pieces of information and record your predictions." Jenny scaffolds student thinking by modeling the procedure in stating, "Your title is, 'Taking Care of Petunias.' I know a little about petunias. I know that they are colorful flowers. But I don't know where to plant them and how much water they need. I think I might learn some tips for planting them and keeping them healthy as I read further in the text, " Jenny says, as she records the information on the "What do you . . ." chart.

What do you . . .		
know?	**want to know?**	**think you will learn?**
Petunias are colorful flowers	• Where are they planted? • How much water should they get?	Tips for planting and taking care of petunias

"Go through your own prewrite and do what I just did using the chart for prereading," instructs Jenny. "Be sure to think like a *reader*." Students begin recording their information and making predictions as Jenny attends to individual striving readers to monitor understanding and offer support. She continues meeting with other individual readers in turn.

After five minutes, Jenny states, "Now I want you to think like a writer again. Paying attention to what you have written in your charts will allow you to write about what your readers may want to know and think they will learn by reading your text. This will allow you to write your informational text with the purpose of providing new information to your readers." She also reminds them to reread often to clarify their writing and to purposefully write information that may meet the needs of their intended reader audience. She continues conferencing with individuals for the next 20 minutes or so while students write.

Jenny invites students to exchange their drafts with a partner for review to collect feedback. She instructs the readers to individually follow the DW-TA process and begin with a prereading using a new "What do you . . ." chart for the texts. She encourages them to continue the DW-TA by reading and recording post-reading comments.

After ten minutes, Jenny instructs students to return their notes and drafts to their partners. She provides time for students to rewrite and reread their own drafts to make appropriate changes. The writers' workshop concludes with students reading their drafts to their table groups. After all interested students have shared their drafts, Jenny states, "Remember that writing like a reader and reading like a writer allows you to become better at both reading and writing."

Text Suggestions

- *Don't Take Your Snake for a Stroll* by Karin Ireland
- *The Everything Machine* by Matt Novak
- *I Wanna Iguana* by Karen Kaufman Orloff
- *Princess Pigtoria and the Pea,* retold by Pamela Duncan Edwards
- *The Twelve Dancing Princesses,* retold by Rachel Isadora
- *Waking Beauty* by Leah Wilcox
- *Who Invited You?* by Candace Fleming

Extension Ideas

★ A modification of this activity could assist writers in looking critically at their writing or the writing of peers. Instead of using a "What do you . . ." chart to record feedback, teach students to use a three-letter acronym chart:

Already knew that!	**AKT!**
Didn't know that!	**DKT!**
WOW! That's amazing!	**WTA!**
Want to know more!	**WKM!**

★ The appeal of this activity is that it mimics acronyms students use in texting, such as LOL! (laugh out loud) or OMG! (oh my gosh). Students can fill in the information that fits into those categories into a chart, or they could mark their text (or the text of their peers) with sticky notes or garage sale stickers labeled with those acronyms.

★ A book like *Waking Beauty* by Leah Wilcox and a modified DW-TA chart allows writers to listen to a text like writers, respond to the text like writers, and apply this experience to their own writing. Students could be given a large piece of construction paper to use at their desks while they listen to *Waking Beauty* being read aloud. They construct their own version of a DW-TA chart, writing the following categories on the paper, and filling in the blanks at various teacher pauses in the story.

What I think will happen	What did happen	Was I correct?
The prince will find a dragon	It was a snoring princess!	No!
He will wake her up with a kiss	He yelled at her to wake up	No!
He tries to wake her up another way	He tried to wake her up with a cannon	Yes!

After the book sharing, the class can discuss whether readers like to be right in their predictions, whether writers want readers to be right, and how students plan to use these ideas in their writing. Writers can have their partner readers fill out the above chart with their own writing to see if they are accomplishing their writing goals.

CHAPTER 6

Viewing Strategies

Television, video streaming, computers, and mobile media devices illustrate how communication and learning have become predominantly visual. Given the prominent role that media plays in our society, children need to be taught how to critically view and how to visually represent ideas.

Visually viewing is the communication process for *receiving* and *interpreting* television and video images, text illustrations, environmental advertisements, computer graphics, maps, charts, graphs, and other forms of media. *Visually representing* encompasses the other side of viewing and includes *creating* illustrations, print media, Web pages, computer images, and artistic representations like acting and sculpting. Most children show interest and engagement in interacting with and manipulating visual texts. Capitalizing on students' interests and the abundance of visual stimuli, we present these five reasons for teaching visually viewing and visually representing to enhance the reading acquisition of striving readers.

★ *Viewing is one way children learn.* Children learn by being able to understand graphic representations of information. Creating activities for nurturing the ability to interpret visual texts allows teachers to capitalize on the spatial intelligence of students.

Reading Skills	Story Mapper	Cereal Book	Caption Writer	Going Graphic	Visual Scavenger Hunt
reading interest	●	●	●	●	●
seeing text as accessible	●	●	●	●	●
fluency				●	
predicting			●		
summarizing		●	●		
connecting	●	●	●	●	●
questioning			●		●
synthesizing	●	●	●	●	●
inferring			●		
visualizing	●	●	●		●
monitoring comprehension	●	●	●	●	●
determining importance	●	●	●		●
listening comprehension				●	
gathering facts	●	●		●	●
social vocabulary			●	●	●
academic vocabulary	●	●	●	●	●
sequence of events	●	●		●	

Figure 6.1. Visually viewing and representing teaching strategies and the reading skills they nurture

★ *Children translate ideas through viewing.* Artistic representations offer a medium for children to make sense of the world. Children are constantly exposed to visual imagery from infancy. This viewing experience provides background knowledge for understanding ideas and concepts through alternative visual representations like those depicted through art.

★ *Viewing supports reading comprehension.* A picture walk can be used to familiarize a reader with a text by exploring its structure and illustrations. Linking the written text with illustrated text can influence a reader's comprehension.

★ *Visually representing information supports reading comprehension.* Having students represent information before, during, and after reading using graphic organizers increases their understanding of what is read. The visual depiction of information allows readers to interact with the text by clarifying, questioning, connecting, synthesizing, and determining the importance of ideas.

★ *Visual representations allow students to display understanding.* Visual representations allow alternative means for students to share their understanding after reading. Striving readers can display their learning through posters, pictures, or computer-created images.

With these reasons in mind, we showcase five ways to use viewing and visually representing to enhance reading ability. Figure 6.1 shows these visual teaching strategies and the skills they elicit.

STORY MAPPER

Description: A story map provides one way for readers to interact with a story by charting its elements. In its simplest form, the story map involves the use of a graphic organizer to identify story elements of character, setting, conflict, and conflict resolution by presenting brief written descriptions of each in cascading text boxes. Students can use the story map during prereading to map the characters and setting and then make predictions about the problem, events, and resolution. Or, they can use the map to keep track of story elements and the events as they occur during reading. Teachers can also have students use the graphic organizer as a post-reading strategy to recap the entire story as a form of retelling and as an assessment of reading comprehension. The story map is a versatile tool that may be used in multiple ways.

The Story Mapper activity provides one highly engaging way for striving readers to attend to story elements and track their understanding. Students draw pictures, cut and paste pictures from magazines, or use clip art from the computer to keep track of story elements and events as they occur. Their final product may look something like a treasure map. Story Mapper allows striving readers to visually represent their understanding of a story for others to view.

Teaching Suggestions

1. State the purpose of the Story Mapper activity: to internalize the structure of stories and to identify a story's main parts—characters, setting, conflict, main events, and conflict resolution—and to visually represent their understanding.

2. Begin with a simple story to model the process for creating a map of the story's elements. You might decide to read aloud or retell a familiar story while creating the map.

3. Invite students to choose an interesting story.

4. Instruct them to prepare all of the materials they will need to create their story maps.

5. Encourage students to read their stories all the way through for the first reading. During the second reading, instruct them to map the story elements by drawing or pasting pictures that identify each story element as they are revealed in the text. Request that they connect each picture with a series of dashes, footprints, and arrows, or in any creative manner that visually represents the story as it unfolds.

6. Once finished, invite students use their story maps to retell their stories to the whole class, a small group, or a partner.

Peering into the Classroom

Lisa begins readers' workshop by telling her second graders, "We have used story maps in the past to show the progression of a story using words. Today you will purposefully use pictures or symbols to help you to better understand what you are reading. Creating visuals will also allow you to show your understanding of a story to others. I will model the process and then you will get to perform Story Mapper on your own."

"You will hear this story three times. First, I am going to read the entire story from beginning to end." Lisa reads the story *The Hair of Zoe Fleefenbacher Goes to School* by Laurie Halse Anderson. During the second reading, she models how to create a story map by drawing a picture of each story element on the whiteboard. She then walks her students through a retelling of the story, pointing to each picture in her map, which depict the characters, setting, problem, four main events, and the resolution. After finishing the retell, she says, "Now it is your turn. You may choose any story that you find interesting."

"I want you to read the story all the way through the first time. Then, during your second reading, you will begin mapping. You may decide to draw the pictures, cut them out of magazines, gather scrap pictures from our art center, or create them using clip art on the computer. Please begin."

After allowing 30 minutes of readers' workshop for students to finish, Lisa invites students to share their visual representations with a partner.

Story Map

Lisa then invites a few volunteers to retell their stories to the whole class. She concludes the readers' workshop lesson by reminding students, "Visually representing your ideas is one way to help you understand any story you read. It will also allow you to show others your understanding as they view your visual representation."

Text Suggestions

- *The Django* by Levi Pinfold
- *Duck Duck Moose* by Dave Horowitz
- *The Easter Egg* by Jan Brett
- *The Hair of Zoe Fleefenbacher Goes to School* by Laurie Halse Anderson
- *Mrs. Spitzer's Garden* by Edith Pattou
- *The Tales of Beedle the Bard* by J. K. Rowling

Extension Ideas

★ One way to extend the idea of using visual elements from a story map is to ask students to create a game board based on their story. Different parts of the game board allow for different ways of visually representing the elements. If the game board was based on *Charlotte's Web*, for example, the game board could be in the shape of a farm, representing the setting. Game pieces could represent the main characters: Wilbur the pig, Charlotte the spider, Fern the girl, Templeton the rat, etc. Conflict and main events could be visually represented by game squares, such as a picture of the fair with a few words describing the plot, like "Wilbur goes to the county fair—move forward two spaces" or "Wilbur doesn't win the blue ribbon—go back three spaces." Resolution could be represented by the final square of the game, with a picture of Wilbur smiling and talking with Charlotte's children. Making a model of this game and reviewing each part could help students understand the visual representation of the story and could get them thinking about how to visually represent the story they read.

★ To accentuate the visual elements of Story Mapper, conduct a class project centered around J. K. Rowling's *The Tales of Beedle the Bard*. Assemble five groups, one for each short story in the book, and assign each group a secret story, instructing them not to share which story they will be representing. Ask them to go through the Story Mapper process for their short story in a manner similar to the one outlined above, but on a large piece of foamboard or chart paper. They will display their story map for the class, and classmates from other groups will attempt to identify which short story from the book they were visually representing.

★ ★ ★

CEREAL BOOK

Description: Book reports are one way for students to show their understanding of narrative and informational texts. They enhance and showcase student understanding by providing a structure for students to identify the elements of a text, summarize

	TITLE OF BOOK (top of box)		
STORY ELEMENTS (left side)	NEW COVER FOR BOOK (front of box)	BOOK REVIEW (right side)	SUMMARY WITH PICTURE (back of box)
	(bottom of box)		

Figure 6.2. Cereal Book Map

important information, and synthesize key concepts. But book reports need not be a chore or a bore, as Cereal Book well illustrates.

Cereal Book provides one way to engage striving readers in purposeful consideration and creative representation of reading comprehension. Students begin by choosing and reading a text. They show their understanding by visually representing literary elements, contents, a review, a summary, and a new cover by decorating the sides of a cereal box.

Cereal Book Activities

Teaching Suggestions

1. Explain the purpose of the Cereal Book activity—to nurture and showcase the students' use of effective reading strategies through a creative visual representation of a text.

2. Invite students to select and read a text of interest. You may want them to focus on a particular genre, specific element(s) of a text, or one or more reading strategies. Students may choose any text within the parameters of the intended lesson, or pick from a collection of texts that you have preselected.

3. Show students a box covered in blank paper or the Cereal Book Map (see Figure 6.2) and explain what each side will include. Or, to keep the activity open-ended for student interpretation, initiate a whole-group or small-group discussion asking students to review the major elements of a book report and/or inviting them to come up with alternatives for showcasing their understanding of story elements and structure. Consider sharing several examples of Cereal Books created by you or previous students.

4. Provide time during readers' workshop, writers' workshop, or individual silent reading over the next few weeks for students to illustrate their understanding of the stories they have read and create their Cereal Books.

5. Invite students to showcase their reading comprehension and expose peers to their texts through brief whole-group, small-group, or partner book talks using their Cereal Books.

6. Display the finished Cereal Books for all students to view.

Alternative Directions

Invite students to measure and cut pieces of paper that match the length and width of each side of the box. Each section may be glued to the appropriate side of the box after they have finished their illustrations.

Peering into the Classroom

Gail's fourth graders are learning comprehension strategies for reading and understanding narrative texts. To support student thinking, Gail models and guides student practice by teaching striving readers to ask themselves what strategies they use to solve problems they encounter while reading. She decides to enhance student understanding of six general reading strategies by having them create a Cereal Book.

Gail begins by explaining the purpose of their readers' workshop mini-lesson by saying, "Today you will be practicing using the reading strategies you have been learning about by focusing on six particular strategies," explains Gail, as she points to the "Six General Reading Strategies" chart she has displayed on posterboard, large enough for all to see.

Six General Reading Strategies

- Use background knowledge/make connections to previous learning
- Visualize what is happening in the text
- Determine the most important ideas
- Draw conclusions
- Evaluate the text/provide a personal response
- Summarize the information

Figure 6.3. Six General Reading Strategies

"The purpose of today's lesson is to practice using these six comprehension strategies while reading a narrative text of your choice. During or after you finish reading your text you will get to extend your thinking and show your understanding as you create a Cereal Book, a visual representation of your understanding for others to view," Gail explains.

"Here are two options for covering your Cereal Books," says Gail, as she shows students one empty cereal box covered completely with poster paper. "You may decide that you want to illustrate the story that you have read by drawing and writing right on a box like this." She then presents another uncovered box that includes six precut pieces of blank drawing paper that match the dimensions of each of the six sides of the box. "Or, you may decide to create each part of your text on a piece of paper that will be glued to the box after you complete it," Gail explains.

"What do we put on each side of the box?" Yolanda asks.

"You will be using each of the six reading strategies listed on the "Six General Reading Strategies" chart to determine what to put on each side. You must visually represent your ideas as much as possible. You may write a little information, but most of your ideas need to be represented through drawings or pictures. For example, you may decide to create a picture of a scene in your text for the front of the box. This would align with the strategy that reminds you to visualize what is happening in the text. As long as you use these strategies to guide your thinking and can explain why you have decided to show your thinking in the way that you do, any representation you decide to create will be acceptable," Gail clarifies.

"Could I draw pictures of other stories that this text reminds me of on the back of the box?" asks John.

"Why would you do that?" Gail inquires.

"Well, that would show my background knowledge and the connections that I make with other books that I have read," explains John.

"Yes, that is wonderful reasoning, John," replies Gail with a smile. "Now that you know what to do, you will need to choose an interesting book or continue reading one that will allow you to practice these six reading strategies and visually represent your thinking. You may decide to read the entire text and complete your Cereal Book after by referring back to the text. Or, you may want to visually represent your text as you are reading by jotting down ideas or quick sketches on the Cereal Book Map that is available for you in the art center. You may begin reading a great story."

Gail circulates around the room to assist individual striving readers and answer questions. Occasionally she brings the whole class together to answer repeated questions and clarify expectations.

Over the next few weeks, Gail conferences with students to monitor understanding and strategy use. She listens to students explanations of their illustrations and the reasoning behind their creation. Gail offers instructional support as necessary and continues conferencing with each student in turn.

As students finish their Cereal Books, Gail invites them to present their thinking through brief book talks in small groups. Completed Cereal Books are displayed in a special area of the classroom for students to view at their leisure. Gail reinforces student learning by saying, "Using these reading strategies helps you to think and solve problems while you read. Using them helps you to interact with the text. By visually representing your thinking and viewing the representations of others, you show your understanding—and understanding is what reading is all about."

Text Suggestions

- *Artemis Fowl and the Time Paradox* by Eoin Colfer
- *Farm* by Elisha Cooper
- *The General* by Janet Charters
- *Journey to the Bottomless Pit* by Elizabeth Mitchell
- *The Perfect Gift* by Mary Newell DePalma
- *While the World Is Sleeping* by Pamela Duncan Edwards
- *The Wings of Merlin* by T. A. Barron

Extension Ideas

★ Another idea that allows for visual representation is to allow students to make actual maps that represent ideas from the book. The book *Journey to the Bottomless Pit* by Elizabeth Mitchell is one that lends itself well to this idea. To visually represent the elements in this text, students can construct a map of Mammoth Cave, leaning on the events and descriptions in the text for support. Students can use each of the six reading strategies, with stress put on visualizing the events, deciding which events are important enough to be illustrated on the map, and summarizing the information. Small pictures could be drawn near each place, representing the events that happened there.

★ Invite students to construct a mobile to visually represent their story. The mobile can focus on any one of several elements such as characters, pictures that convey the setting, or story events.

CAPTION WRITER

Description: Children experience much of their world by viewing pictorial and illustrated representations of it. Such visuals allow children to learn about the world around them as they translate ideas through viewing. In order to accurately translate images, children must be taught how to view them. They must be taught strategies for making sense of what they think they see, based on background knowledge and experience, and what an image really means. Therefore, linking illustrated text to written text can enhance a child's understanding of images.

Caption Writer is one way for striving readers to learn how to accurately interpret visual images like pictures and illustrations in texts. Students view a descriptive image of an animal, an occurrence in nature, or an event. They read supporting literature that explains the image. Students then compile and condense the information to create a brief caption describing the image.

Teaching Suggestions

1. Collect a wide variety of unusual images and illustrations or have the students do the collecting. Scaffold student support by providing pictures that have captions, pictures embedded within written texts, and pictures that stand alone.

2. State the purpose of Caption Writer. Viewing images can be very informative but viewing often requires the support of written text to accurately interpret an image's true meaning. This activity links visual information with written information to enhance the understanding of the viewer and reader.

> ### Scaffolding Support Through Group Work
>
> *Allow students to work in pairs or triads to capitalize on students' strengths and support individual student needs.*

3. Distribute one image with an accompanying caption to each student.

4. Invite students to study their images and think about them. After a few minutes, invite students to turn-talk-and-listen to a neighbor as they explain their images. Circulate the room to listen in on student conversations.

5. Tell students that a caption is a brief explanation of an image. Inform them that they will use their viewing and reading skills to create a caption for an interesting image.

6. Distribute one image without a caption to each student.

7. Instruct students to view the image to figure out its meaning.

8. Encourage students to read the supporting literature to gain understanding of

the image. Circulate the room to make sure that individual striving readers can independently read the supporting texts, to monitor their understanding of the activity and their reading, and to offer instructional support as necessary.

9. Invite students to create a brief, descriptive caption that accurately defines their image. Assist individual striving readers as necessary.

10. Encourage students to share their captions and images by posting them in a special area of the classroom for others to view.

Peering into the Classroom

Jerry begins the lesson by telling his third graders, "Images are all around you. They are a large part of your environment and an important part of the texts that you read. Just like written text, images provide you with information. Therefore, it is important that you are able to accurately interpret those images to understand your world and the things that you read. Caption Writer," says Jerry, pointing to the title written on the board, "is an activity that will help you to make sense of images by using the support offered by written text. You will use reading to help you to accurately interpret visual images in texts," Jerry explains. "Let me show you what I mean."

Jerry continues by distributing one image that includes a caption to each student. "Silently view your image for a moment. Try to figure out its meaning," he says. Jerry models the process by studying his own image carefully. After a few minutes, Jerry says, "Turn-talk-and-listen to a neighbor as you explain what your picture is about." He circulates the room to listen in on student conversations. He encourages individuals to read the captions for assistance if they have not done so by asking, "What does the caption tell you about the picture?"

After a few minutes, Jerry states, "A caption is a brief explanation of an image. With a show of thumbs, indicate if reading the caption helped you to understand what your image is about." Many upturned thumbs show that most students found their captions helpful. Jerry makes a note of three students with downturned thumbs.

"This time you will use your viewing and reading skills to accurately interpret an image and create a brief caption describing it," Jerry explains. He passes out another image to each student. But this time, the images do not have captions.

"Hey, my image doesn't have a caption," Chad states. "How am I going to create one that tells about the image?"

Guided Groups

Identifying several students with a common need allows the teacher to form a group to offer focused instructional support.

"That is an excellent question, Chad," Jerry answers. "By reading the information in the supporting text, you will be able to accurately define the picture and create a brief caption to depict its meaning," says Jerry, as he passes out the supporting information for students to begin viewing and reading.

Jerry provides the same image and supporting text to the three striving readers who showed downturned thumbs earlier. He shows them another image and asks them to explain what it means. He then reads the caption and engages them in a brief conversation. Jerry encourages the three striving readers to work together on interpreting a new image.

Jerry circulates the room, attending to other individual striving readers to assess their ability to read the supporting text independently, monitor their understanding of the activity, and offer support as necessary. He confers with other individuals, guiding their efforts and offering instructional support. As students begin to create their captions, Jerry inquires about the accuracy of their information by asking, "Where did you find that explanation of the image?"

As students complete their captions, Jerry invites them to post their images and captions on a bulletin board for their peers to view and read. Jerry concludes the lesson by stating, "Viewing an image may help you to understand it, but viewing the image and reading supporting information for it can help you to more accurately interpret an image's true meaning."

Text Suggestions

- *Ballyhoo Bay* by Judy Sierra
- *Extreme Scientists: Exploring Nature's Mysteries from Perilous Places* by Donna M. Jackson
- *Fangs!* by Heather Dakota and Tammi Salzano
- *Global Warming* by Seymour Simon
- *Guess Again!* by Mac Barnett
- *Kisses on the Wind* by Lisa Moser
- *The Magic School Bus and the Climate Challenge* by Joanna Cole
- *Outside and Inside Snakes* by Sandra Markle

Extension Ideas

★ Creating captions can help students understand many concepts embedded within a variety of content areas. For example, studying Martin Luther King Jr. during social studies, students can create captions to coincide with pictures depicting significant events in his life (e.g., peacefully protesting, delivering speeches).

★ Consider using a text such as *Guess Again!* by Mac Barnett to look at visual representation from another angle. The written clues to the object are on one page and visual clues with the outline of the object are included in the picture on the other page. Once the first few pages have been examined, readers see that this book is intended to go beyond the obvious and they question their first reaction to a visual representation. Lead students in a discussion of what the author does in the book to trick the reader with visual and written clues, and then ask them if they would like a chance to be as tricky as the author, creating their own pages to form a similar tricky class book.

GOING GRAPHIC

Description: Thumbing through a picture book and "reading" the pictures are natural behaviors for emergent readers. Telling stories of their experiences and making up stories from their imaginations are also natural. When combined, all of these experiences nurture children's development as readers.

Going Graphic is one way for striving readers to capitalize on picture viewing and storytelling to acquire reading. It allows striving readers to develop story sense, use relevant background knowledge, predict, determine the importance of ideas, and draw conclusions. In Going Graphic, students study the pictures in a wordless picture book and determine what each picture means with respect to the progression of the story line. After perusing the entire text, a child creates a logical story to go along with the pictures, practices telling his or her story, and narrates the story to others.

Teaching Suggestions

1. Gather and display wordless picture books with varying numbers of pictures per page.
2. Inform students that they will get to "read" these books by viewing the pictures to create the story. Tell students that the purpose of the activity is to learn how to view *pictures* and practice creating their stories. Remind them that readers use this same process when preparing to read the *words* of a text aloud for an audience.

3. Model the procedure for the whole class or for smaller groups of striving readers.

4. Engage students in a discussion of the story before, during, and after reading, if appropriate.

5. Match individual striving readers with an appropriate wordless picture book according to strengths, interests, and needs. Note that some picture books have multiple pictures per page, whereas others only have one picture per page.

6. Encourage striving readers to take a "picture walk" through the book, stopping to make predictions and asking questions to identify unfamiliar objects or scenes. Encourage readers to go through the entire book to build understanding of the story as a whole.

7. Invite striving readers to begin developing the story when ready and to practice telling it.

8. Ask individual students to tell their stories to you during conferencing. Also encourage students to tell their stories during partner or buddy reading. Invite students to sign up for a time to tell their stories to the whole class in the author's chair.

Peering into the Classroom

Brad gathers his first graders on the rug before him for their routine story time. A traditional buzz of excitement flows through the students. Brad cradles the book of the day in his arms and with a broad smile as he says, "Today we are going to do something a little different for story time. I am not going to read a big book for you to see all of the words, or read a picture book without showing you the pictures to boost your ability to create pictures in your mind, or tell you a story using props. Today I am 'Going Graphic.' I am going to show you a book page by page and I want you to view it silently and we'll talk about it later. Okay?" Brad asks.

"Okay!" students chime in unison.

Brad holds up *Cool Cat* by Nonny Hogrogian. He turns each page slowly, making sure that each student can see the pictures. He takes his turn to view each picture as well. Brad delights at the excitement growing in students as they realize the book has no words. They examine each page with craned necks and wide eyes and can hardly wait to see what happens next. Brad finishes showing the book, saying, "I want you to turn-talk-and-listen to a neighbor quietly to discuss what you noticed," says Brad. The classroom erupts with hushed voices. Brad listens in on student conversations to gather their thinking.

After a few minutes, Brad says, "Okay, what did you see?"

"There aren't any words in that book," says Jenna.

"Yeah, it was only pictures. Cool pictures!" Rylan adds.

"Great observation!" Brad comments. "This is a wordless picture book and today I am going to model how to read it with an activity called Going Graphic.

"Cool!" students reply.

"I have looked through this book a number of times to make sense of the pictures and to figure out my version of the story. I have practiced telling the story several times and would like to tell you the story now," Brad explains.

Brad begins by reading the title and the name of the author from the front cover. He then turns through the book slowly as he tells his story, making sense of each picture and the characters that are introduced. He concludes his story and shares, "You will get to read a wordless picture book and make up your own stories to go along with the pictures. Please return to your seats and I will pass out the books."

Once students are seated, Brad passes out the texts, which he has matched to individual students. Students begin thumbing through their books.

Brad brings the class together, saying, "Please be sure to use your reading strategies as you explore your books. Try to understand what is going on, and create and practice your stories." He then circulates the room to attend to individual striving readers and offer support as necessary.

After approximately 20 minutes, Brad says, "I would like you to practice listening and telling your stories with a partner." He navigates his way from pair to pair to listen in and monitor student understanding. Brad writes anecdotal notes on individuals to help inform future instruction. He wraps up the lesson by saying, "It looks and sounds like you are using your viewing skills and understanding of story to create thoughtful stories. You can sign up on the calendar to share your stories during story time over the next few weeks."

Text Suggestions

- *Cool Cat* by Nonny Hogrogian
- *Mama* by Jeanette Winter
- *The Marvelous Misadventures of . . . Fun-Boy* by Ralph Cosentino
- *Mouse Around* by Pat Schories
- *Rainstorm* by Barbara Lehman
- *The Snowman* by Raymond Briggs
- *Treasure Bath* by Dan Andreasen

Extension Ideas

★ To ensure all students' success, choose a wordless book such as *Treasure Bath* by Dan Andreasen that has fewer pictures. Extensive modeling and scaffolding attempts may be exactly what the hesitant reader needs to take off with this activity.

★ Provide a variety of examples of comics for students to explore and discuss what background knowledge readers need to have to understand the comic, the role prediction plays in comprehension, and what conclusions can be drawn from them. Take away the speech bubbles from several comics and discuss whether the story can be told from just the pictures. Ask students to fill in the blank text bubbles with their own words.

VISUAL SCAVENGER HUNT

Description: Connecting previous experiences and background knowledge heightens learning, as does extending reading to real-life experiences. Creating authentic and interesting viewing experiences before, during, and after reading helps readers to understand new information. Allowing readers to visually represent their comprehension makes it more concrete.

Visual Scavenger Hunt provides one way to enhance striving readers' understanding of what they have read through viewing and visually representing. In this activity, students read about objects or concepts (e.g., fire alarms, friendship). Students then embark on a visual tour of the classroom, school, or playground to identify examples of objects or concepts. To extend and show understanding, students take digital pictures or sketch examples of their discoveries.

Teaching Suggestions

1. Locate objects or concepts shown in a book in your own school environment. As you locate a few examples while perusing the school building, take a photo and/or draw a picture to show students how to complete their Visual Scavenger Hunt.

2. Prepare clipboards with blank paper and/or digital cameras for student use during their search.

3. Explain Visual Scavenger Hunt and its purpose—to help students understand what they are reading about and to allow them to show their understanding. Striving readers will look around the classroom, school, and playground to identify

and sketch or photograph objects that depict vocabulary from a text they have read.

4. Invite students to read the text.

5. Showcase key vocabulary that students will search for in their Visual Scavenger Hunt. Model how to identify or record vocabulary of interest during reading.

6. Pass out clipboards or cameras to students.

7. Invite students to begin their scavenger hunt in small groups with the help of parent volunteers. If there are no volunteers, you may need to lead the scavenger hunt as a whole-class activity.

8. Support students by pointing out or questioning them about possible examples. You might say, "Hey, this looks like an example of an object described in our text. What do you think?"

9. Invite students to share their pictures and sketches and post them in the classroom for others to view.

Pre-teaching Vocabulary

Scaffold student understanding of important vocabulary by teaching the vocabulary words before reading. This will allow them to better understand the text during reading. You can show images of vocabulary words, act them out, or simply discuss key vocabulary terms.

Peering into the Classroom

Wendy's second graders have been learning about inventions in science. She plans to have them read a magazine article in *SuperScience* (Scholastic, 2010) to learn about simple machines. Wendy believes that the Visual Scavenger Hunt will enhance student understanding of simple machines. She performs a brief tour of the school to make sure that many simple machines are evident. She takes a digital picture of some machines and sketches a few examples of others. She will use these to model the procedure for students. She then gathers several digital cameras and clipboards with blank paper for her students to visually represent the simple machines they identify.

Wendy begins the science lesson by saying, "Today, while you continue to learn about inventions, you will conduct a Visual Scavenger Hunt. After you read an article about simple machines, you will travel around the school to identify and sketch or take a picture of simple machines described in the text. The purpose of the scavenger hunt is to help you understand what you have read and to show your understanding through drawings or pictures."

"Where will we find examples?" Daniel asks.

"You'll look for examples of simple machines around the school. Here are two," Wendy answers. She projects a digital picture she took during her tour and says, "This is a picture of a simple machine called a *lever*. What is this picture of?" she asks, showing a sketch she made on her tour. "Turn-talk-and-listen to a neighbor to determine what it is." Students identify the object immediately and explain their thinking to one another while Wendy circulates the classroom and listens in.

"What is the object in the picture?" she inquires.

"A door handle," respond students.

"That's right!" Wendy replies.

She displays another visual representation of a lever found on her tour, this time as a drawing. Students follow the same process as before to determine the object.

Miguel asks, "What is a lever?"

"I'm glad you asked," replies Wendy. "A lever is one of the five simple machines that you will read about in the article." She turns and writes the names of the five simple machines on the board large enough for all to see. Pointing to the list, she explains, "These are the five simple machines you will read about. When you come to each one when reading the text, I want you to underline the word and its definition." As she distributes the magazines, she says, "You may read the text with a buddy and I will come around to answer any questions that you might have."

Wendy navigates her way to striving readers to monitor their understanding of the assignment and the reading of the text. She offers instructional support as necessary and moves to other reading pairs in turn.

After 15 minutes Wendy passes out digital cameras and clipboards to each student pair. She explains the purpose of the scavenger hunt by reminding students that they are to sketch or take a picture of examples of the five simple machines that they find around the school. Students begin the scavenger hunt with Wendy guiding the way. She navigates from each pair to assess understanding and offer support by pointing out objects and questioning students about what simple machine each might be.

After approximately 20 minutes, students return to the classroom and share their findings. Wendy invites students to display their visual representations, grouped by category, in a special area of the classroom. She concludes the lesson by saying, "You certainly found some interesting and accurate examples of these simple machines. Connecting information that you are reading about with real-life examples is a great way to help to you understand what you are reading and seeing."

Text Suggestions

- *Can You See What I See? Treasure Ship* by Walter Wick
- *Cromwell Dixon's Sky-Cycle* by John Abbott Nez
- *Hooray for Inventors!* by Marcia Williams
- *Inventions* by Glenn Murphy
- *What's the Big Idea?* by Stephen Krensky

Extension Ideas

★ Another way to use visual representations to motivate readers is to have them create or capture a visual image of an interesting object. Then provide texts where students can discover pertinent information about their images.

★ The scavenger hunt could also be switched up to allow students the chance to visually represent abstract ideas, like emotions. After reading a book like *Today I Feel Silly* by Jamie Lee Curtis or another book that talks about emotions, moods, or feelings, students could use cameras to capture representations of those feelings. For example, "lonely" might be represented by a student standing alone on the playground.

References

Allen, R. V. (1976). *Language experiences in communication*. Orlando, FL: Houghton Mifflin.

Atwell, N. (2007). *The reading zone*. New York: Scholastic.

Baker, L., & Wigfield, A. (1999). Dimensions of children's motivation for reading and their relations to reading activity and achievement. *Reading Research Quarterly* 34: 452–77.

Caldwell, L., & Ford, M. (2002). *Where have all the bluebirds gone? How to soar with flexible grouping*. Portsmouth, NH: Heinemann.

Clay, M. (1979). *Reading: The patterning of complex behavior* (2nd ed.). Auckland, New Zealand: Heinemann.

Clay, M. (1995). *What did I write? Beginning writing behavior*. Portsmouth, NH: Heinemann.

Coiro, J. (2003). Reading Comprehension on the Internet: Expanding our understanding of reading comprehension to encompass new literacies. *The Reading Teacher* 56: 458–464.

Common Core Standards Initiative. (2010). Washington, D.C: Council of Chief State School Officers and The National Governors Association for Best Practices.

Cullinan, B. (1992). *Read To Me: Raising Kids Who Love to Read*. New York: Scholastic.

Darling-Hammond. (2010). *The Flat World and Education: How America's Commitment to Equity will Determine our Future*. New York: Teacher's College Press.

Edmunds, K. M., & Bauserman, K.L. (2006). What teachers can learn about reading motivation through conversations with children. *The Reading Teacher* 59: 414–24.

Eliot, L. (1999). *What's going on in there?* NY: Bantam.

Erekson, J.A. (2010). "Prosody and Meaning." *Reading Horizons*. 50(2), 80–98.

Farris, P.J. & Werderich, D.E. (2011). *Language arts: Process, product, and assessment for diverse classrooms*. Long Grove, IL: Waveland.

Freeman, D., & Freeman, Y. (2007). *Between worlds: Access to second language acquisition*. Portsmouth, NH: Heinemann.

Goodman, K. S. (1979). Reading: A psycholinguistic guessing game. In H. Singer & R. B. Ruddell (Eds.), *Theoretical models and processes of reading*. Newark, DE: International Reading Association.

Graves, D., & Hansen, J. (1983). The author's chair. *Language Arts 60*(2), 176–183.

Hansen, J. (2001). *When writers read*. Portsmouth, NH: Heinemann.

Harris, T.L., & Hodges, R.E. (1995). *The literacy dictionary*. Newark, DE: International Reading Association.

International Reading Association. (1996). *Standards for the English language arts*. Newark, DE: International Reading Association.

Jones, S. (2006). *Girls, social class, and literacy: What teachers can do to make a difference*. Portsmouth, NH: Heinemann.

Loban, W. (1963). *The language of elementary school children* (Reading Research Report #1). Champaign, IL: National Council of Teachers of English.

McKenna, M.C., Labbo, L.D., & Reinking, D. (2003). "Effective use of technology in literacy instruction." In *Best Practices in Literacy Instruction*, 2nd ed. L. Morrow, L. Gambrell, and M. Pressley, 307–31. New York: Guilford.

McLaughlin, M., & DeVoogd, G. (2004). *Critical literacy: Enhancing students' comprehension of text*. NY: Scholastic.

Opitz, M., & Ford, M. (2001). *Reaching readers: Flexible and innovative strategies for guided reading*. Portsmouth, NH: Heinemann.

Opitz, M. F., & Zbaracki, M. (2004). *Listen hear!* Portsmouth, NH: Heinemann.

Opitz, M. F. (2007). *Don't speed, read!* NY: Scholastic.

Opitz, M. F., & Ford, M. (2008). *Doable differentiation*. Portsmouth, NH: Heinemann.

Opitz, M.F., & Ford, M.P. (2006). Assessment Can Be Friendly! *The Reading Teacher 59*(8), 814–816.

Opitz, M.F., Rubin, D., & Erekson, J.A. (2011). *Reading Diagnosis and improvement: Assessment and instruction*. Boston, MA: Pearson.

Schendel, R. K. (2010). *Voices of striving elementary readers: An exploration of the enhancement of struggling reader research through portraiture methodology*. UMI Online Dissertation Publishing.

Stauffer, R. G. (1970). *The language-experience*

approach to the teaching of reading. NY: Harper & Row.

Thames, D. G., Reeves, C., Kazelskis, R., York, K., Boling, C., Newell, K., & Wang, Y. (2008). Reading comprehension: Effects of individualized, integrated language arts as a reading approach with struggling readers. *Reading Psychology 29*(1), 86–115.

Veatch, J. (1979). *Reading in the elementary school.* Hoboken, NJ: John Wiley & Sons.

Vygotsky, L. (1962). *Thought and language.* Cambridge: MIT Press.

Wolvin, A., & Coakley, C. (1996). *Listening.* (5th ed.). Madison, WI: Brown and Benchmark.

Yellin, D., Blake, M. E., & DeVries, B. A. (2004). *Integrating the language arts.* Scottsdale AZ: Holcomb Hathaway.

Children's Literature Cited

Ahlber, A. (2010). *Everybody was a baby once.* New York: Puffin.

Alexander, M. (2009). *Max and the dumb flower picture.* Watertown, MA: Charlesbridge.

Allen, K. M. (2003). *This little piggy's book of manners.* New York: Henry Holt.

Anderson, L. H. (2009). *The hair of Zoe Fleefenbacher goes to school.* New York: Simon & Schuster.

Andreason, D. (2009). *Treasure bath.* New York: Henry Holt.

Asch, F. (2008). *The Earth and I.* Orlando, FL: Harcourt Brace.

Auch, M., & Auch, H. (2009). *The plot chickens.* New York: Holiday House.

Bagert, B. (2005). *Giant children.* London: Puffin.

Banks, K. (2008). *Max's dragon.* New York: Farrar, Straus and Giroux.

Barasch, L. (2009). *First come the zebra.* New York: Lee & Low Books.

Barnett, M. (2009). *Guess again!* New York: Simon & Schuster.

Barron, T. A. (1998). *The wings of Merlin.* New York: Tor Books.

Bell, C. (2009). *Itty bitty.* Somerville, MA: Candlewick.

Berger, C. (2010). *Forever friends.* New York: HarperCollins.

Blumenthal, D. (2007). *Charlie hits it big.* New York: Harper Collins.

Bluthenthal, D. C. (2003). *I'm not invited?* New York: Simon & Schuster.

Brett, J. (2010). *The Easter egg.* New York: Putnam Juvenile.

Briggs, R. (2002). *The snowman.* New York: Penguin.

Browne, A. (2005). *My mom.* London: Doubleday.

Burleigh, R. (2009). *Clang! clang! beep! beep! listen to the city.* New York: Simon & Schuster.

Burton, V. (1978). *The little house.* Orlando, FL: Houghton Mifflin.

Burton, V. (2006). *Mike Mulligan and his steam shovel.* Newberry, FL: Sandpiper.

Butterworth, C. (2006). *Sea horse: The shyest fish in the sea.* Somerville, MA: Candlewick.

Carle, E. (2008). *The rabbit and the turtle.* London: Orchard Books.

Carol, L. (2001). *The jabberwocky and other poems.* New York: Dover Publications.

Charters, J. (2010). *The general.* Surrey, England: Templar Books.

Clement, N. (2008). *Drive.* Honesdale, PA: Front Street.

Cohen, I. (1998). *A-B-C discovery!* New York: Dial.

Cole, J. (2010). *The magic school bus and the climate challenge.* New York: Scholastic.

Colfer, E. (2009). *Artemis Fowl: The time paradox.* New York: Puffin.

Collard, S. B. III. (2008). *Science warriors: The battle against invasive species.* New York: Houghton Mifflin.

Compestine, Y. C. (2009). *Boy dumplings.* New York: Holiday House.

Cooper, E. (2010). *Farm.* New York: Orchard Books.

Cooper, F. (2008). *Willie and the all-stars.* New York: Philomel Books.

Corwin, J. (2009). *Your backyard is wild!* New York: Puffin.

Cosentino, R. (2006). *The marvelous misadventures of . . . Fun-Boy.* New York: Viking.

Covert, R. (2009). *Me and my animal friends.* New York: Henry Holt.

Crum, S. (2009). *Thunder-boomer!* New York: Clarion Books.

Curtis, J. L. (1998). *Today I feel silly: And other moods that make my day.* New York: HarperCollins.

Cyrus, K. (2005). *Hotel deep.* New York: Harcourt.

Dakota, H., & Salzano, T. (2007). *Fangs!* New York: Scholastic.

Davies, N. (2008). *Surprising sharks.* London: Walker.

DePalma, M. N. (2010). *The perfect gift.* New York: Alfred A. Levine Books.

DiPucchio, K. (2008). *Sipping spiders through a straw: Campfire songs for monsters.* New York: Scholastic.

Drummond, A. (2008). *Tin Lizzie.* New York: Frances Foster Books.

Edwards, P. D. (2010). *Princess Pigtoria and the pea.* New York: Orchard Books.

Edwards, P. D. (2010). *While the world is sleeping.* New York: Orchard Books.

Elliott, D. (2009). *Finn throws a fit.* Somerville, MA: Candlewick.

Elya, S. M. (2011). *Bebé goes to the beach.* Orlando, FL: Harcourt.

Falwell, C. (2008). *Butterflies for Kiri.* New York: Lee and Low.

Feiffer, K. (2009). *Which puppy?* New York: Simon & Schuster.

Fleischman, P. (2009). *The Dunderheads.* Somerville, MA: Candlewick.

Fleming, C. (2009). *Who invited you?* New York: Atheneum.

Fleming, M. (2004). *The bug book.* New York: Scholastic.

Fleming, M. (2004). *A verb for Herb.* New York: Scholastic.

Florian, D. (1997). *In the swim.* New York: Harcourt Brace.

Foxworthy, J. (2009). *Silly Street.* New York: HarperCollins.

French, V. (1993). *Caterpillar, caterpillar.* Somerville, MA: Candlewick.

Friedman, D. (2009). *Star of the week.* New York: HarperCollins.

Gaiman, N. (2009). *Crazy hair.* New York: HarperCollins.

Gervais, R. (2005). *Flanimals.* New York: G. P. Putnam's Sons.

Gorbachev, V. (2009). *Molly who flew away.* New York: Philomel Books.

Graber, J. (2009). *Muktar and the camels.* New York: Henry Holt.

Gravett, E. (2009). *The odd egg.* New York: Simon & Schuster.

Greenberg, D. (2002). *Don't forget your etiquette!* Glen Falls, NY: Red Fox.

Greene, E. (2008). *Mother's Song.* New York: Clarion.

Griffiths, A. (2008). *The big fat cow that goes kapow.* New York: Square Fish Books.

Grimes, N. (2008). *Barack Obama: Son of promise, child of hope.* New York: Simon & Schuster.

Haduch, B. (2001). *Food rules!* New York: Puffin.

Hardinge, F. (2007). *Well witched.* New York: HarperCollins.

Harley, B. (2008). *Dirty Joe the pirate.* New York: HarperCollins.

Harper, L. (2009). *Snow! snow! snow!* New York: Simon & Schuster.

Hatcoff, I., Hatcoff, J., Hatcoff, C., & Uhlich, G. R. (2007). *Knut: How one little polar bear captivated the world.* New York: Scholastic.

Hayles, M. (2009). *Bunion Burt.* New York: Margaret K. McElderry.

Hegamin, T. (2009). *Most loved in all the world.* Orlando, FL: Houghton Mifflin.

Helakoski, L. (2008). *Woolbur.* New York: HarperCollins.

Helakoski, L. (2010). *Big chickens go to town.* New York: Dutton Juvenile.

Henkes, K. (1996). *Lilly's purple plastic purse.* New York: Greenwillow Books.

Hoberman, M. A. (2002). *The looking book.* New York: Megan Tingley Books.

Hodgkinson, L. (2009). *Smile!* New York: HarperCollins.

Hogrogian, N. (2009). *Cool cat.* New York: Roaring Book Press.

Hopkins, L. B. (2009). *Incredible inventions.* New York: Greenwillow Books.

Horowitz, D. (2009). *Duck duck moose.* New York: Putnam Juvenile.

Horton, J. (2006). *Hippopotamus stew and other silly animal poems.* New York: Henry Holt.

Ireland, K. (2003). *Don't take your snake for a stroll.* Orlando, FL: Harcourt.

Isadora, R. (2009). *Hansel and Gretel.* New York: G. P. Putnam's Sons.

Isadora, R. (2009). *The twelve dancing princesses.* New York: G. P. Putnam's Sons.

Isadora, R. (2009). *The ugly duckling.* New York: G. P. Putnam's Sons.

Jackson, D. M. (2009). *Extreme scientists: Exploring nature's mysteries from perilous places.* New York: Houghton Mifflin.

Janeczko, P. (2009). *A kick in the head.* Somerville, MA: Candlewick.

Kann, V., & Kann, E. (2007). *Purplicious.* New York: HarperCollins.

Karas, G. B. (2010). *Young Zeus.* New York: Scholastic.

Karlins, M. (2009). *Starring Lorenzo and Einstein too.* New York: Dial Books.

Katz, A. (2007). *Don't say that word!* New York: Margaret K. McElderry Books.

Keane, D. (2009). *Bobby Bramble loses his brain.* New York: Houghton Mifflin.

Kooser, T. (2010). *Bag in the wind.* Somerville, MA: Candlewick.

Krensky, S. (2008). *What's the big idea?* Watertown, MA: Charlesbridge.

Lamme, L. (2009). *Once upon a Saturday.* New York: HarperCollins.

Lechner, J. (2009). *The clever stick.* Somerville, MA: Candlewick.

Lehman, B. (2007). *Rainstorm.* New York: Houghton Mifflin.

Levine, E. (2007). *Henry's freedom box.* New York: Scholastic.

Lewis, J. P. (2009). *The underwear salesman.* New York: Ginee Seo Books.

Lewis, P. O. (2003). *The Jupiter stone.* Berkeley, CA: Tricycle Press.

Lord, C. (2010). *Hot rod hamster.* New York: Scholastic.

Markle, S. (1998). *Outside and inside snakes.* New York: Aladdin.

McDonald, M. (2005). *Beetle McGrady eats bugs.* New York: Greenwillow Books.

McDonald, M. (2009). *It's picture day today!* New York: Atheneum.

McDonald, M. (2009). *Stink-o-pedia.* Somerville, MA: Candlewick.

Medina, T. (2009). *I and I.* New York: Lee and Low.

Miller, B. (2009). *One fine trade.* New York: Holiday House.

Miller, H. L. (2008). *This is your life cycle.* New York: Clarion.

Mitchell, E. (2004). *Journey to the bottomless pit.* New York: Scholastic.

Moore, L. (2002). *I'm small and other verses.* New York: Walker Books.

Mora, P. (2006). *¡Marimba! Animales from A to Z!* New York: Houghton Mifflin.

Moser, L. (2009). *Kisses on the wind.* Somerville, MA: Candlewick.

Moss, L. (2001). *Our marching band.* New York: G. P. Putnam's Sons.

Murphy, G. (2009). *Inventions.* New York: Simon & Schuster.

Myers, J. (2008). *The puzzle of the platypus.* Honesdale, PA: Boyds Mills Press.

Negron, R. (2008). *The greatest story never told.* New York: HarperCollins.

Nez, J. A. (2009). *Cromwell Dixon's sky-cycle.* New York: G. P. Putnam's Sons.

Nivola, C. A. (2008). *Planting the trees of Kenya.* New York: Frances Foster Books.

Norton, S. (2009). *The girls' book of excellence.* New York: Scholastic.

Novak, M. (2009). *The everything machine.* New York: Roaring Brook Press.

O'Callahan, J. (2009). *Raspberries!* New York: Philomel Books.

O'Conner, J. (2008). *Fancy Nancy: Bonjour, butterfly.* New York: HarperCollins.

O'Connor, J. (2010). *Fancy Nancy: Poet extraordinaire!* New York: HarperCollins.

Oppel, K. (2009). *The king's taster.* New York: HarperCollins.

Orloff, K. K. (2004). *I wanna iguana.* New York: G. P. Putnam's Sons.

Palatini, M. (2009). *Lousy rotten stinkin' grapes.* New York: Simon & Schuster.

Pattou, E. (2001). *Mrs. Spitzer's garden.* Orlando, FL: Harcourt.

Peirce, L. (2010). *Big Nate: In a class by himself.* New York: HarperCollins.

Pinfold, L. (2010). *The Django.* Somerville, MA: Candlewick Press.

Pinkwater, D. M. (1993). *The big orange splot.* New York: Scholastic.

Plourde, L. (2010). *Field trip day*. New York: Dutton Juvenile.

Polacco, P. (2001). *Mr. Lincoln's way*. New York: Philomel Books.

Polacco, P. (2009). *The butterfly*. New York: Puffin.

Polacco, P. (2009). *In our mothers' house*. New York: Philomel Books.

Portis, A. (2007). *Not a stick*. New York: HarperCollins.

Rappaport, D. (2008). *Lady Liberty*. Somerville, MA: Candlewick Press.

Rawlinson, J. (2009). *Fletcher and the springtime blossoms*. New York: Greenwillow Books.

Reynolds, A. (2010). *Back of the bus*. New York: Philomel.

Richmond, M. (2007). *I love you so . . . .* Minneapolis, MN: Marianne Richmond Studios.

Rockwell, A. (2008). *Big George: How a shy boy became President Washington*. New York: Harcourt.

Rosenthal, A. K. (2009). *Little oink*. San Francisco: Chronicle Books.

Rowling, J. K. (2007). *The tales of Beedle the Bard*. New York: Scholastic.

Salas, L. P. (2009). *Stampede!* New York: Clarion Books.

Salzano, T. (2010). *Poison!* New York: Scholastic.

Sawyer, K. K. (2010). *Harriett Tubman*. New York: DK Children.

Schnur, S. (2002). *Winter: An alphabet acrostic*. New York: Clarion Books.

Schories, P. (1993). *Mouse around*. Toronto, ON: HarperCollins Canada.

Schubert, I., & Schubert, D. (2005). *There's a crocodile under my bed!* Rotterdam: Lemniscaat USA.

Schubert, I., & Schubert, D. (2008). *Like people*. Honesdale, PA: Boyds Mills Press.

Schubert, L. (2010). *Feeding the sheep*. Dongguan City, China: Toppan Leefung.

Scieszka, J. (2009). *Robot Zot*. New York: Simon & Schuster.

Shetterly, R. (2008). *Americans who tell the truth*. New York: Puffin.

Sierra, J. (2009). *Ballyhoo Bay*. New York: Simon & Schuster.

Simon, S. (2010). *Global warming*. New York: HarperCollins.

Smith, C. R. Jr. (2008). *Winning words: Sports stories and photographs*. Somerville, MA: Candlewick.

Smith, L. (2010). *The inside tree*. New York: HarperCollins.

Solheim, J. (2001). *It's disgusting and we ate it!* New York: Aladdin.

Spinelli, E. (2008). *The best story*. New York: Penguin.

St. George, J. (2008). *Stand tall, Abe Lincoln*. New York: Philomel Books.

Thomas, J. (2009). *Rhyming dust bunnies*. San Diego, CA: Beach Lane Books.

Tolstoy, A. (1998). *The gigantic turnip*. Cambridge, MA: Barefoot Books.

Torrey, R. (2009). *Almost*. New York: HarperCollins.

Turner, P. S. (2009). *The frog scientist*. New York: Houghton Mifflin.

Van Allsburg, C. (2006). *Probuditi*. New York: Houghton Mifflin.

Van Laan, N. (1992). *Possum comes a knockin'*. New York: Dragonfly Books.

Viorst, J. (2009). *Alexander and the terrible, horrible, no good, very bad day*. New York: Antheneum.

Voake, S. (2009). *Insect detective*. Somerville, MA: Candlewick Press.

White, E. B. (2001). *Charlotte's web*. New York: HarperCollins.

Wick, W. (2010). *Can you see what I see? Treasure Ship*. New York: Scholastic.

Wilcox, L. (2008). *Waking beauty*. New York: G. P. Putnam's Sons.

Williams, M. (2005). *Hooray for inventors!* Somerville, MA: Candlewick.

Wilson, L., & Hillenbrand, W. (2007). *Whopper cake*. New York: Simon & Schuster.

Winner, C. (2004). *Everything reptile: What kids really want to know about reptiles*. New York: Northwood.

Winter, J. (2006). *Mama*. Orlando, FL: Harcourt.

Winters, K. (2003). *Abe Lincoln: The boy who loved books*. New York: Aladdin.

Wishinsky, F. (2000). *Nothing scares us*. New York: Scholastic.

Worth, V. (2007). *Animal poems*. New York: Farrar, Straus and Giroux.

Integrated Language Arts Lesson Plan Form

Objective: _____

Text(s): _____

CONSIDERATIONS	TEACHING NOTES
Before Reading	
Grouping Technique (*check all that apply*): __ whole group __ individual __ small groups of ____ Language Arts (*check all that apply*): __ listening __ speaking __ reading __ writing __ visually viewing __ visually representing Teaching Strategy (ies):	
During Reading	
Grouping Technique (*check all that apply*): __ whole group __ individual __ small groups of ____ Language Arts (*check all that apply*): __ listening __ speaking __ reading __ writing __ visually viewing __ visually representing Teaching Strategy (ies):	
After Reading	
Grouping Technique (*check all that apply*): __ whole group __ individual __ small groups of ____ Language Arts (*check all that apply*): __ listening __ speaking __ reading __ writing __ visually viewing __ visually representing Teaching Strategy (ies):	